Freedom from Lust

Freedom from Lust

Wallace W. White

Writer's Showcase
San Jose New York Lincoln Shanghai

Freedom from Lust

Writer's Showcase
an imprint of iUniverse, Inc.

For information address:
iUniverse, Inc.
5220 S. 16th St., Suite 200
Lincoln, NE 68512
www.iuniverse.com

All Bible quotations are from The Holy Bible, Revised Standard Version, A.J. Holman, Co., Philadelphia, 1962.

ISBN: 0-595-24383-5

Printed in the United States of America

To Philip, David and Trenton. May you each achieve the sweet freedom from the bondage of lust.

Contents

PREFACE

It is no secret that American males have a significant problem with sexually explicit materials. The widespread availability and use of pornography by boys and men has become a major issue in American society and in relationships between men and women. At the root of the growing addiction to sexually oriented magazines, videos and computer smut is a foundational sin: lust.

How the modern Christian male handles the power of lust in his life may be the single most important determinate of his spiritual and social success as a husband, a father and as a Christian generally. The destructive power of lust in our society is probably responsible for more sexual and physical abuse of women, wives and children than we may ever be able to comprehend.

The Bible defines lust in very specific terms. The scriptures give examples of the ruinous consequences of this sin. The Bible also provides us answers to how we might find relief from this sin and from its consequences.

Why are we Christian males so broadly unsuccessful in finding relief from lust? Why are we able to find victory over fears, anger, covetousness, and so many other sinful weaknesses, but stumble when faced with lust? Why do so many committed Christian men move along in their spiritual growth and discipleship until frustrations from sexual lust bring them to a point of defeat and even possible rejection of their faith?

I have found that most men, including most Christian men, do not understand the power of this sin in their lives. In addition, since so many men are reluctant to even discuss this subject, they have not even begun a course of study, prayer and action that could lead them to better understanding. As a friend once said to me when I told him I was considering leading a study for men in the Sunday school on the topic of lust: "Why? Do you want it to go away?"

Who am I to author a book on ways of identifying and overcoming sexual sin? My first career (I am a second career pastor) was in public library administration. I spent nearly 30 years in the field of print and visual publications and witnessed first hand their impact on people. As a Sunday school teacher and active lay Christian leader during those years I developed a curriculum on dealing with lust. Those classroom teachings grew into workshops on this topic for youth and young men. Now as a pastor in the Friends Church, I am increasingly aware of the impact of mental sexual sin on men, marriages and families. This book is part experience, part study and part testimony. Most of all, this work is an attempt to pass along the insights the Lord has given me over the past 25 or more years as I have struggled and prayed to understand this powerful force at work in myself. It has been through His revelation and His wisdom that I have achieved, through His provision, daily freedom from the power of lust in my own life.

It is my personal belief and my personal testimony that we Christian men will not find release to be the men God wants us to be—that we cannot find true victory and creativity in our lives—until we find victory over sexual lust. It is my hope and prayer that this volume will help you find the blessed contentment that comes with freedom from lust. So, it is to those men I address this book: Christian men who find themselves either addicted to pornography or are finding it difficult to break away from regular use of sexually explicit materials. If you are truly ready to begin addressing this problem, I believe the path to freedom from lust laid out in this volume will help you walk away from this problem.

A special thanks to Charlie Rhyan, Dan Broaddrick, Marc Quinter and my son Phil who have given me extra encouragement to commit this material to print.

Wallace White
Delaware, Ohio

1

GOD'S FIRST COMMANDMENT

I t would appear that God intends that most men should marry. The Lord's first commandment to the first generation man and woman was "Be fruitful and multiply" (Genesis 1:28). Generations later when the population of the earth had been destroyed by water, God was preparing Noah to jump start humankind once again. God's commandment to Noah was the same as to Adam and Eve: "Be fruitful and multiply" (Genesis 9:1).

Along with his unequivocal intention that we should be dedicated to the propagation of our kind, God provided a framework in which this reproduction should take place. The scripture probably most often repeated at wedding ceremonies is Genesis 2:24: "Therefore a man leaves his father and his mother and cleaves to his wife, and they become one (flesh)."

From "the book of beginnings" we can see that our Creator has ordained that we be about the task of guaranteeing that there will be another generation to follow us. He also makes it clear in Genesis (and in some New Testament teachings, as well) that it is within the bonding of the marriage relationship that such "multiplying" should take place. It is biblically certain that the Lord has designed us to engaged in the sex act to provide for the sustaining of the human race. It is equally clear that the act of sexual intercourse is to be protected and maintained within the committed vows of marriage. Therefore, it must be his intent that most men should marry.

Teachings against sexual relations outside of marriage are basic to both the Old Testament and the New. The sin of adultery, sexual intercourse by a married person with someone other than his or her spouse, is condemned as sin (Exodus 20:14, Leviticus 20:10, Matthew 5:27, Romans 13:9). Fornication, sexual intercourse between two people who are not married (regardless of whether they are married to anyone else or not) is also condemned as sin (Acts 15:20, 21:29; Romans 1:29; I Corinthians 5:1; 6:13).

We must believe that this scheme, this system of our Creator is complete in and of itself. People are created with a sexual nature. Humans are designed to reproduce. We are to keep the act of reproduction within the bounds of marriage. Within this system God has included the key elements for our highest level of sexual fulfillment. When we stray beyond these basic intentions of our Creator, it is then we begin not only transgressing God's plan for us, but we also begin falling into sexual activities and patterns which reduce and frustrate the highest levels of sexual satisfaction that the Lord intends for us. If a man is ever going to get beyond the frustrations of sexual lust in his life, he must know from the outset that God does have a plan, an environment, a system in place for meeting the sexual needs that he has created within each of us.

Not every man will marry, of course. In fact, Paul's opinion was that we are better off staying single, as he was at the time. Men who are called of the Lord to remain unmarried, for the sake of a ministry or a spiritual service, demonstrate unusual faithfulness in answering that call. Sexual urges and inclinations do not disappear simply because one chooses not to take a wife. The burden for the single, Christian man is learning, under the Lord's leadership, to direct sexual energies into ministries and service to others. All celibates, I am certain, could testify to the significant challenges of redirecting sexual tensions into creative service to others. Given these difficulties, Paul allowed as how most men should probably take a wife: "It is well for a man not to touch a woman. But because of the temptation to immorality, each man should have his own wife and each woman her own husband (I Corinthians 7:1-2)."

The trials of the celibate or single Christian male is another book, which I am incapable of writing. It is my hope that this volume will hold some insights for the single male. My ministry here, though, is primarily to those who are married (or who intend to marry) and are struggling with vicarious sex—sexual pressures which are not easily confined to the marriage bed.

Chapter 10 will go into more detail about God's plan for meeting our sexual needs within marriage. As we begin our move toward achieving freedom from the sexual powers besetting so many of us men today, it is extremely important that we realize that God does understand. Paul encourages us in I Corinthians 10:13 with his knowledge of such a truth: "No temptation has overtaken you that is not common to man. God is faithful, and he will not let you be tempted beyond your strength, but with the temptation will also provide the way of escape, that you may be able to endure it."

When we deal with the power of sexual temptation in the lives of men, we are faced with an impulse, an intense urge, the capacity for which God has created within us. The Bible would seem to indicate that He has created this capacity for intense sexual desires within men for a vital, rather specific reason. Can you imagine what chance we would have of creating the next generation if our Creator had not built into men such a strong mechanism of sexual urges? Without this deep longing for sexual relations, most men would simply spend their lives in front of the television watching football, while their wives whiled away their evenings reading a novel in bed. Yes, the Lord has left us men a wake-up call for procreation by putting within the very being of men what is probably our strongest psychological/physical experience, the sex urge.

This means that the sex urge must be basically, fundamentally good and right. If God has given us this capacity for intense sexual longings, and He intends for most of us to ultimately satisfy these urgings, we should not feel guilty because we are so created. The problem, we will be seeing, is that so many men are not willing and able to let the One who knows what these urgings are all about—the Author of our sex manual, the Bible—lead us in getting our sexuality into a proper place and perspective in our lives. Man's major problem is understanding and corralling these urges into the proper framework. My intention for you men who are wrestling with these urges is to help you find a way to corral this beast.

The man who simply says, "Hey, I'm a sexual animal and just can't help myself," is probably partially right. This does not mean, however, that there is not a way of getting help in putting sex into its proper place in our lives. Our Lord has created this system of human sexuality and has provided adequate provisions for our living successful, productive lives, in spite of the sexual pressures. We fall short because so many of us do not take the time to try to understand the nature of the sin of lust.

2

WHAT IS LUST?

I can recall my first *Playboy* magazine, as if it were yesterday. It was in fact over 40 years ago. I was in junior high school, probably about 12 years old, and a couple of my friends and I were visiting at a girl friend's house. Her father had put a magazine in the magazine rack by his chair without realizing that some adolescent with hormones on parade would be sitting in that chair later that evening. While the group was talking, I began leafing through that magazine, and there it was! A black and white photo of a woman with bare breasts!

I grabbed the magazine and went flying out the front door, into the quiet street, beneath a streetlight. The guys came running out to see what had put me into orbit so quickly. I showed them the picture, and I mean we howled like a pack of young wolves at the sight of that photo.

I ripped the picture out and stuck it in my pocket, then took the magazine back into the house and placed it back in the rack. I carried that folded and refolded photo around in my pocket for most of that summer. The glossy paper was nearly worn through at the folds, and was sweaty from the number of my friends' hands that clutched that picture during that summer of my first discovery of sexual excitement.

What I felt at the sight of that picture was a physical and an emotional kick like nothing I had ever felt before—before puberty. Whatever that jolt was, I liked it, and began scouting the magazine racks of the stores and newsstands in town, trying to find pictures that would produce that same great kick.

I was obviously not the first boy in my family to ever experience such a visual kick. One of my older brothers told me of a time during the 1930s when our family was living on a farm on a mountaintop in West Virginia. As I remember the tale, he was a young teen and had found a "girlie magazine" down in the village one day after school. He took the book of pictures of girls in skimpy bathing suits back up to the farm and hid it in the corncrib. A couple of days later, he went back to that spot to retrieve the magazine for some prime time viewing. It was gone! He knew he had put it in that exact location. How could it possibly have disappeared from such a great hiding place?

The only person that would have had access to that spot during the past couple of days would have been Dad. My brother reasoned that our father must have found the magazine and done away with it. But, he reasoned wrong. You see, Dad was also a healthy male. He apparently happened upon the magazine and removed it to a place in the granary where it could be safely hidden for his own future use. My brother accidentally found the publication in the granary when he was doing some chores, and realized what had probably happened. He swiped it from there and re-hid it where Dad could not find it. By my brother's report, the hiding and finding of that magazine set off a summer-long game of hide-and-seek as he and Dad alternately found and hid the book of photos all over the farm.

For me this is proof that men and boys have really enjoyed photos of lightly clad women since at the least the time of the Great Depression. If full truth be known, I suspect that such sexually provocative photos probably appeared at the time of the development of photography, in the mid-19th century! Certainly the history of painting and erotic illustrations, significantly predating the advent of the camera, gives ample proof that the portrayal and display of the female body, at least for "artistic" reasons, may be nearly as old as the female form itself.

These two generations in my family have not been the last to experience the hidden delights of sexually provocative pictures. When one of my sons was about that same age, his early teens, he posed a tricky question for me. Without much prelude he asked me one day, "Dad, why don't you have a batch of *Playboy* magazines hidden in your closet the way some of my friends' fathers do?" Fortunately the Lord had begun dealing with me about the lust in my life sometime before, so I was able to give that son his first lecture on the harmful and addictive qualities of such magazines.

A few years later I was cleaning up around the tent in the backyard where my son and a couple of his friends had been sleeping out. I found one of the garden-variety porno magazines peeking out from under one of the sleeping bags. Good and reformed father that I was, I quickly carried it off to a safe place in the house where I could later check it out, just for research purposes, of course. I needed to see just how much such publications had changed since I had last seen them! Sounds like the beginning of another hide-and-seek game between father and son, doesn't it? As I recall, I later crunched the magazine well down inside the trash, to keep it away from the other children, and from me.

Why do I share these family stories with you? To show that I understand both through personal experience, and from observations of one generation both ways from me, that lust in the lives of men and boys is amazingly common. It probably always has been, and is probably nearly universal among males. It is active in the lives of boys and men from the time our hormones awaken. According to my father when he was in his 80's (he lived to the age of 93), it continues well beyond our days of physical youthfulness.

So what's the harm? If these sexual feelings aroused in men from viewing the female form are so universal and natural, and they come from a God-created impulse that is intended to guarantee sexual relations between men and women, why should we say anything more? Shouldn't teens and men simply follow their urges and enjoy the hormonal jolt from such sexual desires?

Our civil laws used to condemn adultery, and many moral people today continue to see sex outside of marriage as something we should at least tacitly try to avoid. But what's the big deal about "looking if you don't touch'?"

I believe for our sexual fantasy saturated society the most significant teaching in the scriptures for men is Matthew 5:27-30: "You have heard that it was said, 'You shall not commit adultery.' But I say to you that every one who looks at a woman lustfully has already committed adultery with her in his heart." This is part of Jesus' vital teachings about righteous living, contained in his Sermon on the Mount. It is in this passage that Jesus introduces us to lust. He explains the relationship between lust and adultery, just as he explains in the verse immediately preceding these the relationship between anger and murder. It is with this key teaching of Jesus (especially verses 29-30) that we will begin our effort together to determine what lust is, and to begin building a way of identifying exactly the moment when lust appears in our mind.

Let's start with a garden variety, dictionary definition of the term. Various dictionaries will give a meaning for the word "lust" something like this: "To excite sexual desire" (as a verb); "a desire to gratify the senses; and appetite of the body; extreme or excessive sexual desire, especially the seeking of unrestrained gratification" (as a noun). Lust is the strong desire or craving for something. In general used today, it commonly means the strong sexual passion we feel as we long for something forbidden or unattainable.

The Greek work Jesus used in Matthew 5:28 is epithymeo, the verb form of epithymia, which means "desire" or "longing." Epithymia/epithymeo is translated variously in other New Testament passages as "covetousness" (Romans 7:7; 13:9), "the love of" (money) in I Timothy 6:10, both showing a strong desire for something beyond reach or easy possession. The concept here is that simple desire, when attached by sinful man to that which God forbids, becomes lustful.

Returning to Jesus' teaching, then, he is saying that when a man (and I believe he is specifically talking about males here, not "mankind") looks at a woman in a way as to specifically "excite sexual desire" within himself, he is, in this action, committing a form of adultery with her in his mind ("heart"). Jesus is saying that when I look at a woman in such a way as to feed a bodily appetite, or with extreme or excessive sexual desire, I am committing a sin that is similar to the act of fornication itself.

Strong words! Rather unbelievable, one might say, in this age of sexy photos, television shows, movies and videos, and Internet cybersmut. We can rationalize, "Jesus must have meant something else with this teaching. He could not be asking me to give up that private, harmless, extra long look at the female form!"

I can still recall the time a number of years ago when I began seeing this teaching for what I now believe Jesus actually meant. It was a weekend when I was attending a professional conference (I was a public library director at the time). My conference roommate was a friend who seemed to have a measure of spiritual sense about him. As we were beginning the usual process for such a conference, which would have resulted in a great deal of "girl watching" and probably an adult movie, I shared this scripture with him. His reaction was the same as most men when confronted with Jesus' teaching about lust. He responded, "No, that isn't what Jesus really meant!" But, I was beginning to realize that Jesus was calling me to task for sexual sin in my thought life. I set out that weekend on what would become a 15-year search for peace in my mind and spirit in this matter of lust.

I can see now that Jesus really understood men. He knew full well the way our heavenly Father had chosen to create us. His teaching recorded in Matthew begins with, "Any man who looks at a woman lustfully…" Jesus had a clear fix on the two levels of sexuality of men. Until we understand this aspect of male sexuality, we cannot begin to grasp the debilitating nature of lust.

3

THE TWO REALMS OF MALE SEXUALITY

When we think of the term "sex", we normally think of the physical joining together of man and woman in the act of sexual intercourse. If we stop there in our definition, we miss most of the sexual activity of men. Men, of course, do participate in the physical act, but much of the sex life of men is mental. In fact, most of sex is mental, not physical.

It is certainly no secret that men are sexually stimulated through sight. When I discovered the photo in my first Playboy magazine as an adolescent, I saw something that set my hormones ablaze. There was no touch involved, and there was nothing that I did to excite myself sexually at that moment. I simply looked at the picture and the rest, as they say, is history. In fact, at that innocent age in the early 1950's, I did not even know that such pictures even existed, or at least did not know that they could be within my grasp. The experience was a total, visual, sexual surprise to me.

I do not know how the psychological process works that leads to the visual sexual arousal of men. I really do not have to, since I know that the system works with an immediate, powerful effect. In fact, I have read that the psychological impact on men of being sexually aroused visually is the most powerful, pleasant occasion that the male's system experiences. It may well be stronger, and can overpower such other physical urges as hunger and thirst. I personally believe that is probably true.

I can recall in my younger years going to almost any length to feed that feeling of sexual kick. As an adolescent I stole magazines from the racks of a couple of magazine stores, jut to feed that urge (I was too young to buy them). I have prayed for forgiveness for those thefts. Neither store is any longer in existence, so direct restitution for my thefts has not been possible. Later in life, I have lied to my wife and family in order to sneak off to an adult movie. I ask their forgiveness for those times of deceit.

I can recall a time at a professional conference in Detroit when I first began waking up to the possibly destructive tendencies that feeding this urge was creating in my life. I had finished a long day of meetings and gave into the desire to take in an adult movie. I grabbed a taxi and asked the driver to take me to a theater address I had gotten from the newspaper. He took me into a decaying, dangerous section of that city. I can recall thinking as I stepped out of the safety of that taxi, "What am I doing here? This is a neighborhood where I could get my throat cut!"

The important point here is that the urge for the visual sexual arousal experience was even stronger than my sense of safety and well being. What had led me to go against my own sense of right and wrong and had led me to take such chances? It was not alcohol, or drugs, or prostitution. It was that most powerful of all psychological experiences of men. That sometimes overwhelming urging is what I like to call the "Red Button experience." It is the draw men have to sexual arousal simply by engaging in a situation where we can leisurely observe the female form. It is the deliberate choice we make to push a button deep down in our psyche. At the push of that "Red Button" we get a hormonal jolt that sends our body into excitement and ecstasy and places our mental and intellectual faculties on hold.

I am rather comfortable sharing these degrading personal experiences with you readers only because I have come to understand that many men (including probably many of you readers) have had some similarly unreasonable or risky experiences of your own. You may know the feeling that I am describing. At times some men will give up a good meal, set aside some hobby or otherwise fulfilling activity, just to be able to push the Red Button. It plays out as an almost uncontrollable longing for that feeling that comes only through visual, sexual arousal.

A few years ago the now defunct, quasi-scientific magazine *Quest* reported the results of an interesting study on mice. The specific area of the brain that generates this arousal response in males was identified and isolated in male rats. Electrodes were attached to that section of the brain which permits the release of the hormone involved in this sexual kick. Any time the rat wanted to experience this rush of sexual feeling, he simply had to press a button in his cage using his nose.

Once the male was thoroughly practiced with the button arousal, a sexually available female rat was placed in the cage with him. The purpose of the experiment was to determine whether the male would tend toward choosing the female sex partner or would stay with the button. Guys, I will give you a moment to think about this situation and to guess which the male rat most often chose. It should come as little surprise to many of you that the male most often chose to push the "Red Button." He developed a desire for the rush of sexual arousal over that of the actual sex act with a willing sex partner. This might not come as too much of a surprise to some of you wives, either. Some of you have seen your husbands continue watching the sexy video he brought home, even after you have given him strong signals, like "I'm going to bed...will you be up long?"

What does all of this mean? It is clear that men have two levels of sex life: the visual (psychological) and the relational (physical). The first level is almost exclusively played out in the mind. It is visually fed. It is sexual arousal that does not necessarily involve physical relations with anyone. The second level is the actual sex act, involving full physical contact with a female.

The visual sexual experience for males begins at puberty. Sexual arousal by way of viewing the female body becomes a chief preoccupation of most adolescent boys. In this day of easy pornography, visual sexual arousal has the potential of becoming almost a way of life for boys and young men. I worked in public libraries for a number of years. I could not guess the number of library books and magazines that I have seen defaced by having sexy pictures ripped out. A common experience in libraries also is finding pornographic magazines, which have been carried into the library, stashed in various remote locations of the bookshelves. They are obviously left there by someone who has chosen that private spot to "study" the pictures.

It is easy to assume that most of these vandalized books and magazines and the discarded porno items were the result of adolescent boys' curiosity. But it is important to note that this activity goes beyond simple curiosity. It is essential to our understanding of boys beyond puberty and their sexually explicit materials that we realize that the viewing of such sexually oriented pictures feels wonderful to that young boy. We sometimes hear someone defending a boy looking at such materials say, "He is just curious." The effect of pictures of the female body on a boy goes well beyond intellectual curiosity about how girls are different from him. The effect is an intense sexual warmth and arousal. In fact, there probably is no other physical feeling, to this point in his life, that brings him anywhere near the physical pleasure that this simple viewing of the female form brings. The pleasure reaction to the pictures is so gratifying that he probably will find himself returning to the experience again and again.

You notice that I only include boys in this phenomenon. My number of years of working with adolescents in libraries have shown me that the girls begin turning on to the romance stories at this point in their development, while the boys want pictures. I recall a 5th or 6th-grade girl coming onto a bookmobile one time, closely followed by a few of her giggly girlfriends. She apparently was their developing leader, since she came up to me and said, in a rather husky, adult voice, "We want the books on love!" There seems to be little likelihood that boys from her class would spend much time poring over novels searching for the romantic passages. This is too slow and does not provide much kick. But give him one explicit picture and, POW!

A boy may be intensely involved with sports, or any other school activity. He may find great satisfaction and be developing self-esteem with a successful hobby. But, there is nothing that happens to his body that quite feels as amazingly exhilarating as that video, or that X-rated web site, or just that TV commercial with the bikinis.

In fact, he may be from a Christian home and have been taught a few things about sex. He may understand that sex before marriage and outside of marriage is wrong. He may have been cautioned about some of the of problems associated with masturbation. His parents may well have taken the time to warn him of the life-threatening diseases that can result from casual sexual contact. They may have told him not to watch "dirty movies" and tried to limit his access to computer porn. That young teen may have even made a pledge to himself at that early age that he would avoid sexual contact with girls until he is married. These efforts may help him "stay pure" in his relations with girls. None of this, however, affects or changes how disarmingly wonderful the visual sexual experience feels to him. A firm resolve to avoid physical sexual contact will not necessarily impact on the boy's desire for, and possible addiction to vicarious sex.

Neither parent may have been able to help him understand this feeling, partially because they may not understand it very well themselves. In my talks and workshops I have found that this physical phenomenon is little known to women. Their interest in the details of such feelings in males seems rather short-lived. Men generally seem to me to be still rather confused by these feelings and are often reluctant to discuss them with other men (and certainly not with their sons). Under such circumstances, helping a son come to terms with such sexual arousal activities can be a rather disconcerting experience for either parent. Since parents little understand the nature of he Red Button experience, the subject is often just ignored, and the problem goes unaddressed.

So, with the ready availability of explicit, pornographic materials today, boys have an opportunity to develop this experience of sexual excitement to a rather high level at a rather early age. In fact, this very act of viewing female nakedness or people portraying the sex act in such pornographic materials can become for that young person, sex itself. What I mean is that a boy who has been actively involved with pornography from age 12 or so until the time of his marriage, say in his early 20's, may have had 10 years or more of visual, vicarious sex. By that point he is a fairly good human equivalent of that mouse in the cage. He is still interested in pushing the Red Button, even though he is now in a marriage relationship where "real sex" is regularly available to him.

Pushing the Red Button can become a highly addictive activity. I have heard wives call Christian radio programs featuring the problem of pornography to report that their husband would rather watch "dirty videos" than come to bed with them. Or, she may reveal that a husband would prefer to have physical sex with her when videos or magazines that stimulate him are also available. His two realms of sex is being defined by the visual experience, rather than by the actual physical one.

Let's consider in more detail this second realm of male sexuality, the relational one. When a man and woman reach marrying age and begin their life together as partners, they most typically are not going to bring the same sexual expectations and needs to the marriage bed. What they have come to expect from sexual relations has been molded by a variety of environmental influences since childhood. Each also brings his or her God-created sexual needs. The wife brings her need to be touched and held. She has a natural desire to be romanced. She may have begun practicing and honing those feelings back in adolescence with romance novels and TV soaps. She brings a need for caring, deliberate physical intimacy.

In contrast, the typical husband is pretty much just a male hormone with legs! He can be sexually aroused at a moment's notice, even without any touching. His quick arousal is accompanied by a simple interest in quick release of his sexual tensions. In this frame of mind, he does not make a very effective romantic mate. He is faced with the task of learning the physical and emotional needs of his wife. The new husband must learn to develop patience and a desire to meet her needs. Those are the demands placed on him by relational sex. He must learn to take the needs of a sexual partner into account. But for the past 10 years or so, sex has just meant him and sexual arousal through visual images. "Sex" has been totally selfish, instantaneous, on-call at any time—nothing much to learn, as everything was provided him by natural, sexual impulses. The two realms of his sexuality have now come into sharp conflict. One is practiced and easy, while the other is new, complicated, and sometimes demanding.

Wives, what some of you end up with these days in the form of a husband is a fellow who is stuck at about age 13 or 14 years in his sexual/emotional maturity. Most of these men have made the mistake of trying to figure out what sex is like by learning from the media. Little did he know that the media has long ago discovered the male Red Button. Madison Avenue assumes you can sell anything to guys if you include cleavage. Red Button ads sell beer, soda pop, chewing gum, lawn mowers—nearly any product intended for use by a man. The most curious example of this that I have seen was a calendar on the wall in an auto mechanic's shop featuring a photo of a bikinied model slinking around amidst a batch of chain saws!

That man you are marrying has been bombarded for years by people who want to catch his consumer's eye and who know that nothing works better than pushing his Red Button. Just as a cat cannot easily ignore something making quick movements, and a dog seemingly cannot pass by any disgusting odor, so it seems that we men are fixated by the passing glimpse of a slightly clad female in an advertisement. The problem is, if you ask most men what product is being sold by a particularly fleshy commercial, they cannot quickly recall the product being sold, just the model and what little she was wearing.

Moms and dads of girls, is there a lesson here regarding your message to them about modesty in their dress? Girls dress to attract the attention of the boys. That's normal, but a sense of balance and modesty is important, too. Girls need to understand that deliberately revealing too much of her body through her wardrobe selections is counter-productive. Boys are easily attracted to the partially clad female form, but her body becomes the object of admiration, not her (as a person). The healthier relation results from the charm of personality (coupled with fashionably tasteful dress) attracting the boy's attention. He will tend to remember the face and the person, not just the body. Ultimately, he will also tend to choose to marry the girl with this type of appeal, rather than the one who is just interested in sharing her shape.

By the time you women get us as husbands these days, we have been so lambasted with sexually-explicit stimuli, including the ocean of images to which we have chosen to expose ourselves, you are faced with a man whose sense of sexuality is quite immature. Sex for him is most likely a highly visual, impulsive and self-gratifying experience.

It is in this context of lust's potential damage to the marriage relationship that we see the insipid danger of lust. It may also suggest why Jesus equated it with actual adultery. Lust is a self-centered experience. We can even see active lust as an effort by men toward a form of sexual independence.

Our age has an exaggerated view of independence as maturity. We have a romanticized notion that a personal state of independence from parents, family and all others is the sign we are "grown up." The Marlboro man of cigarette advertising fame, alone on a hillside, astride his horse, or the lonely biker cruising down a deserted country road are too often accepted as the symbols of manhood. Getting along in life alone, within the confines of our own resources, exempt from any need for others is certainly not a biblical view of maturity, nor is it biologically sound.

When we are born we spend our first years almost totally dependent upon our parents and others around us for our daily subsistence. We need their help for food, protection, and for most of everything required to grow and function. We stay in that primarily dependent state until we move toward the adolescent years when we begin growing away from the daily dependence on the energies and attentions that mom and dad have been providing.

The adolescent reaches a point when he does not want to even appear to need his parents. He walks ahead of them at the mall. He tries to lose them in the crowd when they are on hand to see him off on a trip with his youth group. He tries very hard not to have to go to them for advice, but seeks the information freely given by his peers. That young person is reaching the essential stage in his maturation when he begins breaking free from his parents' constant care. That stage of desired independence seems to arrive fully about the time he ships off to college or the military and leaves his parents behind. This separation from childhood dependence is good and necessary. Many parents seem to dread the thought of that time of "the empty nest" arriving, while others see it as another level of maturity for parents. In the argument as to whether life begins at 50 or at 60, someone has said that life begins when the last kid has left home and the dog dies.

The problem is that too many in our society see that stage of new independence from parental control, beginning in adolescence, as the final stage of maturity. The scriptures repeat the ancient truth (from the book of Deuteronomy) in Matthew 22:37 that "You shall love the Lord your God with all your heart, and with all your soul, and with all your mind...and...you shall love your neighbor as yourself." The world assigns the highest level of maturity to those who appear to be self-sufficient and independent. The scriptures assign the highest level of maturity to those who are dependent upon our Lord and who are interdependent with their neighbors (including even their parents). The system of raising children to maturity is completed when we see the young adult turning to a realization that there is a Power beyond his and all other human life, to which he must be accountable. He then returns to the company of his parents like a long-lost friend, seeking advice and sharing experiences adult-to-adult. The human matures from near total dependency to a level of independence from those who raised him, to interdependence with others, to dependence upon the Creator who originally gave him life.

Maturation is stalled when a young man stops at the adolescent level of assumed self-sufficiency. The continuing practice of lust in a young man leads him along a path toward an attempt at sexual self-sufficiency. If he adds masturbation to his growing habit of conscious visual sexual arousal, he has a potent combination that is destined to eventually put him into powerful conflict with the relational sexual responsibilities in marriage.

Young brides today are all too likely to be marrying a young man who can withdraw into this one-two punch of visual arousal-masturbation as a substitute for the more demanding intimacy and mutual sex of the marriage relationship. That is particularly likely if her new husband has had a decade or so of developing a psychological dependency on the Red Button experience.

4

CURIOSITY OR LUST?

I f we can assume that Jesus did know what he was talking about when he said that lust is a sin, and that it has much of the same impact and consequence as adultery, how can a man begin to identify in his own life where curiosity ends and lust begins? I argued with God about this for many of my early years as a new Christian. I reasoned that he created in me a necessary curiosity about the female form and that when I watched the girls on the beach, or those in shorts walking down the street, or viewed the magazines and movies, I was merely exercising that God-given curiosity.

There must be a way that each of us can determine in his own mind when he has crossed the line from curiosity over into the sin of lust. I believe that the first chapter of James' letter presents the biblical framework for making such a determination.

Review with me, if you will, verses 12-15 of the first chapter of James.

"Blessed is the man who endures trial, for when he has stood the test he will receive the crown of life which God has promised to those who love him. Let no one say when he is tempted, 'I am tempted by God'; for God cannot be tempted with evil and he himself tempts no one; but each person is tempted when he is lured and enticed by his own desire. Then desire when it has conceived gives birth to sin; and sin when it is full-grown brings forth death."

This important teaching provides the outline for anyone to determine the point at which sin begins. Following James' progression through the process of temptation, desire, sin and death permits us to see the general area of transition from our curiosity to the sin of lust.

James indicates that the first step toward sin is temptation. If something is tempting to us, that means that it is alluring or attractive to us. It attracts our attention. The process of moving from curiosity to lust begins with something that attracts our attention, something that is alluring to us. We are willing to give up our focus elsewhere to pay attention to that object or thought.

If a girl gets out of her car in short-shorts and walks around to the curb side to put money in the parking meter, and a man sitting in the parked car behind spots her, it undoubtedly registers in his mind: "There is a girl in sexy shorts!" She attracts his attention and draws his attention for the moment from whatever else might have been occupying his mind. At that point he has, by chance, only registered the fact of her existence and her physical appearance in his mind. He knows that she is there, and that she is in sexy shorts. So far there is no "desire" involved in this scene. His attention has simply been attracted to something that is quite interesting.

The next step may include his being honestly curious about her: Does he know her; or does he recognize the car that she is in; or is she from here in town? At this level he still has not generated any desire in his heart, just curiosity.

The next step is the crucial moment, according to James. Does he intentionally and purposefully permit a desire to be generated in his mind toward that girl in shorts? ("…when he is lured and enticed by his own desire." vs. 14). Notice that I did not say, does he generate a desire for that girl. He does not need to think, "I would really like to have sex with that girl" to generate a desire in his mind toward her. If he is going to lust for her, all he need do is desire to use her to push his Red Button: to watch her long enough to deliberately get that rush that comes in the male anatomy when he uses his eyes to gain sexual arousal from a woman's body.

James says that we should not blame God for bringing that sexy creature into our path. This would not normally be a "test" on God's part to see if we can be moved toward lust for her. He also says that we should not blame God for that deep longing we have to use her for visual sexual stimulation. The Bible writer states that we begin our steps toward sin when we determine in that moment to use that girl on the street for our own sexual stimulation. When we willfully move toward experiencing a sexual desire either for her, or a desire to use her to excite ourselves sexually, we move from temptation to selfish desire. Some have said it this way: "The first look is curiosity, the second is sin." James would say that the second look is the level at which we intentionally develop a desire for using her in some sexual way. This would be where lust begins.

"Then desire when it has conceived gives birth to sin (vs. 15)." Jesus states in the Matthew 5:28 passage, "I say to you that every one who looks at a woman lustfully has already committed adultery with her in his heart." Once we have chosen to use the woman in the shorts as a means of visual sexual arousal, Jesus, I believe, would say that we have chosen to commit adultery with her in our heart. We have sinned against her and against God. The woman does not know that she has been used, but we do, and God does. Sin has been committed through our intentions and our eyes, and in God's presence. Our working definition of lust, then, could be: intentionally, willfully using a woman, other than your wife, for the purpose of visual, sexual arousal. The incident might involve a real woman, or a picture representation of her.

James goes on to state in verse 15 "…and sin when it is full-grown brings forth death." Can it be possible that such innocent "just looking" could lead to such an end result: death! Sin of any kind, unchecked, leads to death of some sort. Paul warned in his letter to the Romans, "For the wages of sin is death…(Romans 6:23). In the next chapter of that same letter he agonized over the sin in his own life that seemed to overwhelm him at times, and cried out, "Who will deliver me from this body of death?"

We look at these warnings in the scriptures of death resulting from unrepented sin and sometimes wonder if that term "death" is not a bit of an exaggeration. Over the past year or so a woman friend of mine and I have measured our skepticism about these teachings about sin and death against the continuing decline of her former husband into a life of drugs and alcohol. After his recent attempt at suicide and commitment to a mental health facility, the Bible's warning seems considerably less extreme to both of us.

In the Garden of Eden Eve was considering disobeying God's warning not to eat of the tree of the knowledge of good and evil. She was persuaded by the serpent who won her over with the bluff, "You will not die." We often convince ourselves that we surely will not see any kind of death, just because of the sin in our life...certainly not for something as common as sexual sin.

Actual adultery contributes to an almost immediate devastation of the bonds of marriage, a death of the relationship. It is swift and relationally disastrous. Lust differs in that it is a slow, insipid death of relationships, resulting from the man's mind and energies being focused on pushing his Red Button. It also leads slowly to a general break in his relationship with females, in that he increasingly holds them apart from himself as an object for his own visual stimulation and pleasure. With a few exceptions for those girls and women closest to him in his family, he slowly and gradually corrals women in general into that realm of his life where they provide him visual, sexual pleasure. He may "solicit" them for his pleasure either out in public, on the page, or on the screen. That state of awkward, crippled relationship with the opposite sex is death to any male who would hope to receive the abundant life of love, intimacy and sexual relationship that God intends for him as a husband. And, once a man has determined to lust for an extended period of time, after a particular woman, the transition into a loving relationship with her is made extremely awkward. Part of that awkwardness is probably a feeling of guilt for using her in this way. An additional element is the subconscious distance his voyeurism has placed between him and her.

How can we determine the point at which curiosity or "just looking" crosses over into lust? The lessons we can learn from James are:

- We men should learn to control the situations that generate a great deal of sexual temptations for us. The easiest way to avoid the lust experience is to intentionally and intelligently minimize the situations in which we will have to make the decision whether to take the second look or not.

- When tempted by a random cause (such as the girl on the street), we should be put on alert that sin is at hand, and should begin the process of finding protection from that sin. A plan of protection will be discussed in a later chapter.

- If we have given in to "the second look" and it felt good, recognize the result as lust and deal with your actions as sin.

- Seek forgiveness for the sin and so avoid the slow process that leads to death of relationships with women and with God.

5

LUST AND ADULTERY

Many men do not necessarily believe that what we have been discussing is sin. They figure to do a little girl-watching or to read a few magazines and take in a couple of movies or videos is not so bad. It is easy to rationalize these activities and say, "Hey, that is not so bad…it's just normal!" Jesus made a rather strong point about lust in his Sermon on the Mount. He said that it is like committing adultery in our mind. Let's look at some more of the evidence that would indicate that lust and adultery have much in common.

We learn in the Genesis account of the creation of man and woman that they are called together in marriage to "become one flesh" (Genesis 2:24). Our marriage vows often include the additional teaching from Jesus when he said in Matthew 19:6, "What therefore God has joined together, let no man put asunder." The act of becoming "one flesh" in marriage, in the sexual act, is a sacred, God-ordained commitment and bond. The Ten Commandments and the Sermon on the Mount both include the prohibition of breaking that bond by going outside the marriage bed for sexual intercourse (Exodus 20:14 and Matthew 5:27).

It appears that Jesus shows us the truly disastrous nature of adultery when he discusses divorce in Matthew: "And I say to you: whoever divorces his wife, except for unchastity and marries another, commits adultery (Matthew 19:9)." He had said earlier in this chapter that no one should break the bonds of marriage, since they are sealed by God, the creator of the man and woman. His teaching here brings to mind Malachi 2:16: "For I hate divorce, says the Lord the God of Israel."

The prophet was comparing the unfaithfulness of Israel in breaking its covenant relationship to God to a man who breaks the marriage covenant with "the wife of his youth."

Why then would Jesus allow the grounds of adultery as the single basis for one partner to divorce the other? If we see a marriage between two partners as a new entity—a bonding that creates almost a new being—a marriage relationship then has something akin to an identity of its own. It has a life and energy beyond the two people who comprise the marriage partners. Two halves of a whole join together to make the wholeness, the oneness. When either half is ripped away from the other, the life, energy, identity of the marriage between these two is lost. This wholeness was previously consummated and sealed in the sexual relationship between the two partners ("they become one flesh").

When either partner in the marriage turns away from that "one flesh" of their union, the whole of their marriage is traumatized. The oneness is ripped apart, severed like a limb ripped loose from the trunk of a body. The sin of adultery is the mutilation of that body which God creates when a man and a woman agree to being bonded under his creative intentions.

Jesus seems to be saying that adultery is so traumatic to the body of the marriage that he would excuse the offended marriage partner if he or she does not want to endure the long process of reattaching the severed limb to the body. The process of restoring the oneness of the two, when one partner has sought to join with someone else "in one flesh," can be so difficult and painful that our Savior appears to excuse the partner against whom the adultery has been committed from having to stand such agony. Obviously one may choose to endure the restoration/reconciliation process. Many marriages have survived the ravages of adultery, thanks to the sacrifice and patience of the offended partner (and to much counseling). This scripture, though, would seem to give that partner relief, if the partner chooses divorce rather than the work of reconciliation.

How could lust have any similarity to the crippling consequences of adultery? Make no mistake about it, lust is a sexual experience. Earlier we talked about the two realms of male sexuality and saw that visual sexual arousal can actually compete with physical sex for the attention of the husband. If a husband has developed an appetite for "girl watching" or for sexually explicit videos and magazines, he has entered into a sexual exercise that will compete with the actual sex act with his wife.

In my early years as a husband, I can recall planning for trips to other cities for professional conferences. Facing the prospect of being away from my wife for a week or so, it was proper and desirable that we would come together as man and wife prior to those trips. But, I recall my thoughts and plans for the sexually oriented movies I would probably see while I was away, and that greatly dampened my own interest and enthusiasm for being an intimate companion for my wife. This is apparently a common experience among men who have developed a serious taste for vicarious sex.

As I mentioned earlier, various Christian radio call-in programs I have heard on this topic indicate that many wives are aware that the magazines and videos their husbands use have become direct competition for their own times of intimacy with their husbands. This competition would not be dramatically different if those husbands were having an actual affair with another woman—if they were actually committing adultery. The symptoms are quite similar: going beyond his own sex partner for sexual arousal or attempts at satisfaction; indifference to the intimacy and sex needs of his own wife; and a general self-gratification attitude towards sex, regardless of the consequences for his marriage.

God's apparent intention when he created the marriage relationship was that the husband would find his sexual satisfaction in his own wife, period. When God created the portion of the brain that houses the Red Button, it appears to me that he had in mind a mechanism by which the man could be aroused at the sight of his own wife's body toward interest in the sex act. This interest, turned toward sexual intercourse with his wife, would lead to mutual satisfaction and to the pro-creation of a new generation. I seriously doubt if the Lord intended that a society should create an environment in which everyone seemed to be aiming their message directly at the Red Button. Nor do I believe that our Creator had in mind that we men should fix our activities on the sexual self-indulgence of lustful experiences, at the exclusion of an energetic, giving relationship with a member of the opposite sex.

Lust is similar to adultery in that, when it is a regular part of a man's activities, it weakens his interest in his wife (if he is married), or lessens the hope for such an interest when he eventually marries. It turns his sexual center away from the intimacy of his relationship with his wife, and produces a sexual self-gratification mind-set that greatly restricts the essential aspect of mutual satisfaction in physical sex between mar-riage partners.

As God intended that the marriage bed should be kept undefiled, he also seems to intend that our mental sex life does not defile that total bond of self-giving that welds two marriage partners into one flesh. Going outside the marriage for actual flesh, or for only imagined flesh, violates that bond. Adultery is a rapid violation of marriage bonds. Lust is a gradual, insidious violation.

The story of David and Bathsheba in 2 Samuel could be a case study for us on this issue of the relationship of lust and adultery. It is recounted that "When David arose from his couch and was walking upon the roof of the king's house, that he saw from the roof a woman bathing; and the woman was very beautiful. And David sent and inquired about the woman" (11: 2-3).

On the surface it might seem reasonable that David was simply curi-ous about whose wife this woman might be. Any man who has ever experienced the Red Button experience knows intuitively, however, that the sight of this beautiful woman in her bath caused David's hor-mones to go on alert. Now David did not lack sexual activity. The scriptures list at least seven wives prior to Bathsheba, plus sons from various concubines. It would not be very likely that on the day he spied the woman in the bath that he was lonely for female companionship. What would launch David along such a rapid course, leading to his adulterous affair with Bathsheba?

Because he was king, whatever David wanted, David got. He simply followed through immediately, possibly even that very day, from the initial sexual arousal he experienced in seeing her naked. A less powerful man might have settled for the occasional peek from the roof at that same time of day, just for the arousal (voyeurism). This lustful activity might not have led to the adultery and eventual murder of Bathsheba's husband. The fascination with Bathsheba might have led a less powerful man to a gradual lessening of interest in his own wife back on his couch.

Active lust, then, is adultery in miniature. It causes much the same results over a longer period of time. Both the adulterous husband and the voyeuristic husband is involved in a pattern of destruction of his marriage relationship.

Just a brief word here about rape. Rape has often been described as an act of power as much as an act of sexual imposition. King David had the political power to make such a sexual encounter happen, even if the wife of Uriah was not at all in favor of the idea. A demented male personality today, which constantly brings itself under the frustrations of the Red Button, may chose to exercise the power vested in David even though no such power exists for him in our society. If there is an increase in rape in our society, some of the source for such violence must be seen in the increased opportunities for young men to isolate themselves with pornography. Such materials indeed lead to lives of frustration, as well as to withdrawal from healthy social contacts. When coupled with the horrid insinuation in some pornography that women desire to be overpowered sexually, it is apparent that certain of these frustrated, diminished minds will tend to respond in socially dangerous ways. I suspect rape is both an exercise of power and of sex.

6

LUST AND THE DREAD "M" WORD

This would be an appropriate place to take a look at the "dread 'M' word": masturbation. Some have described masturbation as that activity about which few people talk, but in which so many engage. I have found in my workshops that this is the topic most men are simply not going to discuss, so one can just save his breath in encouraging group discussion! Given that level of reluctance, I typically hand out a short printout from some good Christian teachings on the subject, and I let that suffice. A few more words about this deeply secret topic might be helpful here, however, in order to show the devastating one-two punch of lust/masturbation.

The scriptures are rather silent about sexual self-gratification. Some point to Genesis 38: 9-10 as evidence of biblical prohibition of masturbation. The text reports that Onan "spilled (his) semen on the ground, lest he should give offspring to his brother. And what he did was displeasing in the sight of the Lord..." The point in this passage does not seem to relate to masturbation as sin. The teaching, rather, relates to early Hebrew responsibilities between brothers.

Most Christian psychologists I have read on this topic assert that masturbation, in and of itself, is not sin. As an occasional exercise in the release of sexual tensions, it should not be rejected out-of-hand (excuse the pun). Since the Lord's intentions for our sexuality involve so much more than this self-centered act, however, it is an activity that must not be looked on as an end in itself. Masturbation should certainly not be seen as our Creator's sexual goal for us.

Given that most people will engage in the practice of masturbation in their lifetime, and that there is no particular biblical prohibition for the act, why even include the topic in this book? The relationship of masturbation by men in conjunction with the use of sexual fantasy materials would appear to be so common that we must look more closely at that relationship.

It is commonly understood that women can be sensitive to touch nearly anywhere on their bodies. God has given them sensors rather broadly distributed across their bodies. Sensually rubbing or massaging a woman's skin, in nearly any part of her body, will normally result in a pleasant sensation for her. Women not only enjoy the caressing and touching which seems to hold little interest for men, but they also seem to enjoy the giving of caresses nearly as much as they like being on the receiving end.

An aside here, men. You wonder what women enjoy in times of intimacy? Take time to study the covers of romance paperback books at the newsstand. Even though the men on the covers are often baring their manly-man chests and arms, the center of attention most often is what the hero is doing to the heroine's neck or ear. We men are mesmerized by genitalia. Women are especially sensitive to attentions paid to neck or ear, at least according to those wonderful artists who design the romance book covers. Remember, those covers are there to attract women's attention and her money. Do some of those same things, and you may better attract your woman's attention!

Men, I was about to observe before our trip to the book racks, have their sensors rather well centered in our genitals. Gentle rubbing of a man's arm, back or legs does not necessarily result in a pleasant sensation for him. In fact, it is not uncommon for such continuous caressing to be a bit of an irritant for him. Sensation of touch is extremely high, however, in the genitalia. Men do not experience sexual heightening any where else in the body. A small boy begins his sexual experiences in life by "playing with himself," the early sensations of touch to his genitals. That activity holds some regular attention for the boy until he reaches puberty. Once the "juices start flowing" he also discovers the Red Button experience of visual sexual stimulation, and the one-two punch is in place.

It is at this point that our real sexual center, the mind, takes over from the purely physical sexual center, the male genitals. It should come as no surprise to us that these two centers of male sexuality team up to create the fantasy/masturbation cycle for boys and men. The male now has a way of sexual arousal at will (pictures, videos, or just girl watching), and a physical way of releasing the sexual tensions which he has built up (masturbation). This cycle leads to the final sexual experience, an orgasm.

We need to dissect this cycle to see where lust, or sexual mental sin, comes into the picture. You will recall from our discussion of the letter of James that sin enters when a man willfully chooses to use a woman, other than his wife, for the purpose of visual sexual stimulation. The sin in the fantasy/masturbation cycle is not so much in the masturbation, but in the choosing to participate with materials or a scene in which he uses the visualization of the woman's body to push his Red Button.

The use of someone as the object of your sexual arousal constitutes "lusting after her" and committing adultery with her "in your heart." If you do not believe that this mental adultery plays a large role in your acts of masturbation, and that our chief sexual organ is our brain, try the act of masturbation sometime totally free from visual or mental fantasy. We are inevitably drawn to and are sexually energized by an image in our mind, often a re-creation of an image taken from a former lust experience.

In our society where men are surrounded by temptations to lust after women in television commercials, in movies, on the beach, in ceaseless visual messages, it is easy to see that sexual tensions can build quickly. These tensions can build equally fast for the married man as they do for the single man. When the single Christian male builds such sexual tensions, his choices are: "tough it out" and just let it pass, commit sexual sin with someone not his wife, or masturbate. Since actual physical, sexual release with a women is typically relatively difficult for the single man (compared to the married man), the single often falls into a pattern which feeds the fantasy/masturbation cycle. Visual sexual stimulation is exhilarating, which leaves him with sexual tensions, which are pleasurably released through masturbation. This cycle of tension/release may seem like a win-win situation to him, absent a willing female. Both sides of the cycle involve pleasurable feelings. The trap that he is laying for himself, however, goes well beyond the veneer of pleasure.

This brings us to the first problem of masturbation. It is no accident that we refer to it as "self-gratification." It is a self-centered, non-relational, isolating experience that cannot be reasonably substituted for the God-created intentions for our sexuality. We are designed sexually to be in intimate physical and emotional relationship with the opposite sex. The sex act is the culmination of the marriage bond. The man who is caught up in mental, sexual lust and physical self-gratification is moving into a sexual isolation that will limit his healthy relationships with the opposite sex. This cyclical habit can, over time and with its ease of availability, limit his effectiveness in healthy relational sex if he does marry. For this reason, it is my opinion that single men should avoid pornography and the trap of the Red Button with all the faith, power and determination they can muster.

I suggested that these sexual tensions can be created by a married man as well as by a single. The option for releasing these tensions by a husband is normally sexual relations with his wife, which is often available. A second option for the husband is also masturbation, if the wife is "not in the mood," and a third is to "bite the bullet" and let the tensions pass. It is in this decision area that we come to a second problem with masturbation: it can all too often become a substitute for normal sexual relations with a wife.

Just as the Red Button experience as a means of sexual stimulation and exhilaration is an easy and quick method for men to experience sexual arousal, masturbation often becomes a quick and easy release for such self-induced tensions. The young husband who has had several years of Red Button experiences before his marriage may have already fallen into the fantasy/masturbation trap well before his wedding night. If he believes that he can continue this pattern after marriage, and simply entice his wife into the marriage bed each time he has engaged in lustful activities with magazines and movies, he is about to enter into a whole new realm of sexual frustration.

Men can be ready for sexual intercourse in just a few minutes, or even seconds, with the right mental arousal. But what often is a quick mental/physical arousal for men is a slower, more emotional act for women. Wives need to have the sex act come in the context of intimacy, romance and extended periods of touching and foreplay. But, as a modern wife, her attention is often caught up by her job, or the children, or other important issues in her hectic daily life. As much as she longs for times of romance, these times may well fall off her schedule and beyond her energy. In this context, it is certainly not reasonable for a husband to expect his wife to be ever on-call for release of his sexual tensions, especially if he has become adept at regular use of sexually explicit materials for his arousal.

Given that the normal, healthy sexual relationship of today's marriage partners will not include a willing, daily surrender by the wife to a husband who chooses to excite his sexuality through sexual fantasy materials, that husband will too often turn to masturbation as a substitute for the sex act with his wife. He may even believe that she is just not being fair with him. He may grumble that she is just never ready for sex at the same time he is. The truth is, he is engaging in a form of sexual adultery with other women. Jesus would say that he has committed adultery with these women in his fantasy materials, and the masturbation simply seals that adultery: having sex outside of his marriage.

Some men claim that the use of sexually arousing materials makes the sex better with their wives. I challenge that assertion. Sexual arousal that has been gained outside of the physical relationship with a wife is already a form of sexual relationship outside of the marriage. It is also a sexual tension that he brings into the physical relationship with his wife that demands using her for its release. Coming to the marriage bed with sexual tensions at such a heightened level will hardly serve the needs of the women: to be slowly and carefully caressed and aroused. Men who claim that such self arousing before intercourse adds to the marriage bed are simply deluding themselves. It does little or nothing for the sexual satisfaction of the wife. In this way lust has an effect similar to actual adultery outside of a marriage It also is clearly a chief contributor to the common problem of early ejaculation among male sex partners. The truth is that intentionally increasing sexual arousal before sex is simply going to rush the sex act.

When a young man has developed a sense of convenient, quick sexual arousal through the use of pornography, and has settled on a method of quick release of sexual tensions through masturbation, he is going to find it awkward and frustrating to work the intimacy and sexual needs of his new wife into his cycle of easy sex. Do you remember the mouse and the button experiment? You'll recall that the physical button was connected to his Red Button (in the brain). The fantasy/masturbation button for men is probably the human equivalent of the button in the mouse's cage. When faced with a sexually available wife, that husband may tend toward the easier, less demanding, slower route of his visual kick/masturbation release mechanism.

Richard Dobbins of Emerge Ministries in Akron, Ohio has a useful teaching on the topic of masturbation and marriage. In his video series "Building Families That Last" Dobbins asserts in the tape "Love and Affection" that the Bible is silent on this subject. He stresses, however, that some issues may be involved in male masturbation which will make it a biblical issue:

- Use of pornography with masturbation constitutes lustful relations with a woman other than your wife.

- Preference for masturbation to intercourse with your marriage partner is a clear detriment to healthy, physical sexual relations with your spouse.

- Even mutual masturbation between partners should not take the place of regular, genital intercourse.

In saying that the scriptures do not appear to condemn masturbation, I would not want the Christian husband to believe that the Lord has given us free use of self-gratification at will. We will see in a later chapter that it is our Creator's intention that we should be focused on our mate's needs for intimacy and sexual gratification, not merely on our own. A life of continued and casual masturbation easily leads to sexual self-centeredness and isolation. Masturbation as a regular activity can become addictive behavior. Selfish sex is bad for relational sex. Self-gratification is selfish, lonely, isolating sex. It adds nothing to the mutually satisfying sexual relations that our God will make available to us in the marriage bed, if we follow His design.

7

ANGER AND LUST

Several times in the previous chapter I mentioned the frustration that comes when men reach a sexual arousal peak (regardless of the source) and can find no convenient, accessible release. Given this dilemma, a significant amount of the frustration and anger in men can be rooted in the experiences of lust.

I find it particularly fitting that Jesus teaches in his Sermon on the Mount about anger and its relationship to murder before he moves on to the relationship between lust and adultery. Matthew 5:21-22 records, "You have heard that it was said to the men of old, 'You shall not kill; and whoever kills shall be liable to judgment.' But I say to you that every one who is angry with his brother shall be liable to judgment…"

Jesus is saying here if one wants to understand and deal with the roots of murder, he must first understand and deal with anger. He then goes on to say that if we are going to understand and deal with adultery, we must first understand and deal with mental sexual sin. I find that much of the anger in my life has resulted from one of two sources: either frustration, or self-pity. I would suggest that this is probably true with most men.

Just a quick mention of the latter source of anger. Self-pity feels good. The attitude of "the world is not fair….I haven't gotten a fair shake in life" brings about what some used to call "a pity party." When we feel sorry for ourselves, at least someone does! And, the more we languish in self-pity, the longer the anger hangs with us. We get to the point where we really don't want to give up our anger, because it feels good to feel mad. To give up the anger is to give up the pleasant sense of self-support.

Anger is a God-created emotional mechanism for dealing with situations where we have been unfairly treated, but it is also a reaction to situations of frustration. Frustration is a position we find ourselves in when our actions or intentions are thwarted or blocked. If I am trying to replace a nut on a bolt on my car and after several tries I cannot get the threads to engage, I become frustrated. As I continue to try to get the nut started and have no success, I may get frustrated to the point that I fling the nut against the garage wall. This is anger being expressed from a root of frustration.

I can recall as a teenager being so frustrated about something in my life that I threw a punch at a cupboard door and sent it hurling across the kitchen past my surprised mother (it was a very old, weak cupboard, and didn't take much of a punch!). I can recall as a young husband being so frustrated about some situation that I struck what I assumed was a solid cupboard door and found that I could put my fist right through it. I've seemed to picked on a lot of cupboards in my life, probably because they could not fight back.

I can talk about these moments of rage from my earlier years because I know that they are not an unusual experience among men. I suspect many men reading this book could share similar stories, some of which probably make my cupboard stories look rather tame. I can recall many times seeing teenage boys and young men walking around with casts on their hands: evidences of having slugged door jambs, lamp posts, trees, or nearly any other immovable object within reach. Others have chosen targets for releasing their anger which have led to damage and abuse to those people close to them: wives, children, friends. Why do we men do such stupid things? Why are we so much more likely to express anger in such physical ways than are women?

One of the most common forms of frustration shared by men of all ages is sexual frustration. I am certainly no expert in psychology, but from personal experience I can tell you that we men carry a tremendous burden within our lives at times from the weight of sexual arousal. The Lord has done a wonderful job of designing us so that we not only notice the female form, but in permitting a pressure of sexual arousal in us to become so intense that we become rather desperate to relieve those tensions. Men cannot really understand the burden women face in carrying a child and giving birth. In a similar way, women cannot really grasp the pleasure that men experience with visual sexual arousal, nor can they imagine the excruciating pressures within us for a release of those pressures.

The Lord has made the experience of holding her very own baby so desirable to a woman that most will move along the path to a baby in spite of the anticipated pains of childbirth. He has also made the experience of visual sexual arousal so enticingly pleasurable that society cannot help but have a multitude of sexually aroused men walking around looking for a method of relieving the tensions produced by that warm, pleasant experience.

This also means that at any given moment there is a vast legion of males slouching around in frustration from not having suitable release available at the moment. The most natural form of release, and the most desirable one is sexual intercourse. For the single male, that is quite often just a distant dream. For the husband, it might not be the right night. So it is at this period of time (I suppose we could say men have "periods" also, but they are much more frequent than the menstrual cycle of women, and much more erratic) that men are likely to express anger, either verbally or physically.

Men certainly get angry over many other things than sexual tension build up. I believe, though, that much more of the anger expressed by males in our society is rooted in sexual frustration than we might normally suspect. And, the younger the man, the more likely the anger is rooted in such frustration.

Robert Frost wrote in his poem "A Concept Self-Conceived:"

"Forgive, O Lord, my little jokes on Thee
and I'll forgive Thy great big one on me."

Who, other than Frost, knows to what "little joke" he was referring? I have a notion that he was probably pointing up something more existential than this predicament of men facing the pressures of sexual frustrations. But, whatever the poet's intentions, the couplet could well apply to this aspect of a man's life. Men find ourselves in the pinch between being drawn to sexual arousal by stimuli around us, which leads to a pressure to relieve these tensions, which may leave us in frustration from not having such relief readily available. It is not unreasonable to question at times how this "trick" has been played on us.

I suggest that the younger one is, the more likely sexual frustration may be near the source of his anger. As a middle-aged man, I can look back and report that the intensity of sexual frustrations does diminish over the years. In my workshops on freedom from lust I report in jest to the young men in attendance that "I have good news and bad news for you about the sexual frustrations you are experiencing at this point in your lives. The bad news is that it will continue on through most of your life, often well into your elderly years. The good news is that we are all going to die someday!"

Joking aside, we need not be quite this fatalistic. Tendencies toward sexual tensions and frustrations do eventually peak, then diminish into our later years. If the middle-aged man can resist being frightened by the weakening of these feelings in his life, he can gain a whole new level of peace in his relationships. If he panics at the realization that he is not as easily aroused as he used to be and that he does not feel the same level of need for sexual release, he may run around like a fool, trying to regain the same mental sexual edge that he had as a teen or a younger man.

In our younger years, the sexual frustrations regularly become so intense that we may take out our anger in all sorts of socially undesirable ways: punching inanimate objects, picking fights so that we can strike an animate object, racing our car around like we have a death wish, or just generally being a giant pain in the neck to those around us. If someone were to stop the young guy and ask him what he is mad about, he usually would not be able to give a reasonable answer. He would probably not be able to pinpoint the source of his frustration.

One of the added predicaments for men is that these times of sexual arousal come much more easily at times of lowest stress, like our days off or during vacation times. So, these are times when we tend to be around personal friends or family more than during hectic work days. If these frustrations are not relieved or reduced, those closest to us tend to get the force of our anger. Small matters of disagreement between a frustrated man and members of his family can lead to seemingly disproportionate reactions on the husband or father's part.

What does this have to do with lust? It is a given that intense sexual arousal will lead to a sense of need to relieve sexual pressures, through one of the channels discussed earlier. Men who regularly use pornographic materials for arousal expose themselves to the potential of sexual tensions and frustrations for which they may or may not have acceptable, desirable, or convenient methods for release. A dutiful wife cannot necessarily meet the demands of a husband who participates in such a practice.

The regular practice of lustfulness in pushing your Red Button through use of such materials is going to lead to increased instances of frustration, irritability, and anger. The people on the receiving end of those feelings will tend to be those closest to him: his girl friend, or wife, or children, or parents. It would seem foolhardy for a hungry man, who had no immediate hope for food, to spend long periods of time staring at and drooling over tantalizing photos of pot roasts or apple pies. Such aggravation would naturally lead him to frustration and anger. The same can be said for men who pore over pages and pages of naked women in magazines or stare at scene after sexual scene on a screen. This world is not structured in such a way as to relieve all the sexual frustrations they are building up. And, according to Jesus, God never intended for us to hurt and abuse our emotions by such intense and exaggerated use of the sexual arousal mechanism that he has created within us.

The intensity of sexual arousal in men is somewhat seasonal, also, especially for those of us who live in areas of climate changes. The old adage "In the spring a young man's fancy turns to thoughts of love" is pretty much on target. I once heard a man say, "It appears that men have three sins they struggle with most: lust, lust and lust. In the springtime we add a fourth: lust!" Male hormones waking up from the winter doldrums is probably as common among human males as among the lower animals. In olden days, it appears that war was a chosen outlet for such frustrations and aggression. Notice that the scene of David and Bathsheba begins with the observation, "In the spring of the year, the time when kings go forth to battle...(3 Samuel 11:1)." In David's time, and I suspect for centuries after, male hormone energy was probably tied closely to warfare. Thank goodness we have found a few less destructive outlets today!

8

VICTORY OVER LUST

Once we have a reasonable idea of what lust is and at what point it begins in our daily experiences, it is time to move on to determining how we might have victory over this sin. First, however, we must be certain that we want to defeat this sin in our life.

You will recall my story of the man who responded to my suggestion that I would like to lead a Sunday school study on freeing our lives from lust. His whimsical remark to me was, "What, do you want it to go away!?" Our study to this point has shown that the visual sexual arousal experience is one of the most pleasant psychological/physiological feelings that we men can have. Do we want to lose that feeling, that warm rush?

If that "second look" habit in us has taken on too large a role in our thought life, regardless of our age, we as Christian men must take a serious look at our Red Button pushing. Has the visual, sexual arousal habit in my life begun affecting the potential of my full, loving relationship with a girl friend or with a wife? Do I find that I shy away from some personal relationships or social contacts in order to spend more time looking at my magazines or watching my videos? Am I growing toward becoming the righteous, whole person that God has intended me to be, or am I being limited by an overpowering desire to spend time with my sex thought life?

If you can answer "yes" to some of these questions (and I am certain that many of you men reading this book will, as I did at a point in my life, see the power of lust becoming rather overwhelming) I suggest that you bear with me for awhile to see if victory over this powerful sin might not lead you to deeper relationships and a richer life in Christ.

It is recorded that Jesus was once entering Jerusalem and encountered a lame man lying by the Pool of Bethseda (John 5:1-9). When he saw the invalid lying among the many infirmed people, Jesus asked him a rather surprising question: "Do you want to be healed?" The man admitted that he was, in fact, waiting for a healing experience, so Jesus provided him with new wholeness.

I find that the area of sin in my life that seems to be the most resistant to healing is lust. I have heard from other men also who have found victory generally over the power of sin in their lives, but become frustrated and discouraged when they begin dealing with victory over lust, specifically. The term "tap-root sin" or "defining sin" can be used for that sin which runs deepest in one's life (see Hebrews 12:1). This deepest of all habits, dependencies or sins defines the point at which a person is most likely to turn away from God rather than give up this one dependency. Nearly any sin has an intrinsic pleasure or appeal involved with it, but lust seems to me to be the most basic and most appealing of the sins in the lives of most men. In fact, I suspect that if you were to ask groups of Christian men to write down the most common sins in their lives, the large majority would list lust as a chief problem area. It may well be when sin is spoken of generally in conversation, in a sermon, or in any illustration, that most Christian men think instinctively of sexual sin, including lust, for the purpose of defining sin for themselves.

So, the first question for us truly is the one that Jesus asked the lame man: do we really want to be healed of the power of the sin of lust? My hope for you is that you will not reserve this area of your life, away from the healing power of God, and thereby miss the beginning of new depths in relationships and a more meaningful and powerful walk with the Lord. Mankind seems to have been created with several levels of potential life. The most basic, and base, is a life not much above that of the lower animals. When we set as our ultimate goal the mere exercise of our sexual natures, we can get stalled at that lowest human level. Meaningful social contacts, with rich giving of ourselves to others, is a higher level of human existence. Eventual freedom from lust can release us for these types of contacts. The highest level of human existence, what Bernard of Clairvaux called in his book *On Loving God,* "the fourth degree of love" (the highest level of love), is when we lose ourselves (our self) in God's love and take on the characteristics of that love. To settle for a life of simple sexual arousal and fulfillment is to sentence ourselves to the least God has for us.

If I do want to find victory over the sin of lust, where do I begin? Let's look at the remainder of Jesus' teaching in the Sermon on the Mount regarding lust. In Matthew 5: 29-30 we read:

> *"If your right eye causes you to sin, pluck it out and throw it away; it is better that you lose one of your members than that your whole body be thrown into hell. And if your right hand causes you to sin, cut if off and throw it away; it is better that you lose one of your members than that your whole body go into hell."*

Fortunately readers of this passage are generally familiar with the use of exaggeration to demonstrate a point, or many men would be wandering around blinded in one eye or missing an arm! Jesus obviously is not asking anyone to disfigure or dismember himself to rid himself of the sin of lust. He is using this dramatic exaggeration to say that sometimes drastic measures need to be taken when the end result we are dealing with could mean either eternal life or an eternity out of fellowship with our Creator. He is saying that we may well need to take some aggressive steps if we are going to free ourselves of the power of lust.

Since Jesus had said in the verses just before these that to look upon a woman lustfully (to use her for your own Red Button experience) is having adultery with her in your heart, his illustration then of "plucking out the eye" seems very appropriate to his teaching. I believe that he is saying that we need to take away those things from in front of our eyes that are most likely to cause us to be overpowered by the sin of lust.

I would ask you readers: What is there in your daily life that may need to be removed to protect you from those situations where you are most likely to commit the sin of lust? Are there magazines that you buy or subscribe to, but have to hide from your children ("for their protection"), or from your wife (out of guilt), so they will not see them? Are there television shows that you regularly watch because they provide sexual titillation. I like to call those programs "titty Olympics" shows: programs with plots that always involve a great deal of cleavage and bouncing breasts? Does your VCR provide a quick and convenient break from your work week through rental of sexually-explicit videos? When your wife wants to watch a video with you, do you find yourself selecting a raunchy video for the both of you, when she really would rather have something with a little romance, and a decent plot? (Confused about whether your wife really wants to watch X-rated videos with you? Just ask her, and listen!) Do you find an increasing amount of the time you spend on the Internet drifting toward X-rated web sites? Or, if you are a young man and find yourself being drawn to the beach as much as your schedule will permit ("just to work on my tan"), isn't your real motive to check out the babes in the bikinis or thongs?

The first step toward victory over lust is beginning to determine what drastic steps you must take to remove materials and experiences that naturally feed your desire to lust. Pray about this area of your life and let the Holy Spirit illuminate your motives. He will show you why you really use these materials, or why you really go to the beach. We become real experts in rationalizing why we do something, but God's Spirit can cut through the nonsense and show us the true motives for our actions. If you honestly want to begin the healing process toward freedom from lust, you must take stock of what has to go from your daily life: all those things you are using to feed your lust: the magazines, the television shows, the videos, the unfiltered Internet access, and the locations where you go for the specific purpose of looking at female flesh.

David gives a testimony of his intentions to keep the personal spaces of his life free from that which offends God.

> *I will walk with integrity of heart*
> *within my house;*
> *I will not set before my eyes*
> *anything that is base.*
> *I hate the work of those who fall away;*
> *it shall not cleave to me (Psalm 101: 2b-3).*

In David's time "setting something base before his eyes" probably meant objects of worship of foreign gods. In our time, however, this promise to our Lord can mean eliminating any items that hold a strong draw for us toward some sin. For most of us men the base and degrading things we need to keep out of our view involve sexually explicit materials. Just as we are tempted by such strongly attractive objects, David found the same problem when he left his house and went out on his roof. With hindsight, he probably should have included his roof as a place where he would seek protection from that which drew him away from righteousness. His spying Bathsheba in her bath came beyond the safe and comforting protection of the space in his house that he had tried to keep free of temptations.

I know that this first step is a tough one. I have been through this inventory, and I have found it extremely difficult, if not impossible in our own strength, to remove all the items I had previously put there to help push my Red Button. I have known and counseled alcoholics, and a favorite ploy of the recovering alcohol abuser is to hide bottles around the house, for those times when he knows he will want to fall off the wagon (often out of self-pity).

It seems to me at times that our society is specifically trying to defeat me in this issue of freeing my personal environment of lustful materials. One does not need to have a very broad involvement with our popular culture to be daily bombarded with sexually explicit images. I cannot recount all the times I have gone to the Lord shouting, "God, this is impossible!" His answer has always come back swiftly: "With men this is impossible, but with God all things are possible" (Matthew 19:26). What the Lord has consistently shown me in dealing with lust is that I cannot find victory over lust in my own strength and wisdom. I am totally dependent upon him for his provision in this area, much the same way "12-step groups" (like Alcoholics Anonymous) teach their adherents that they cannot overcome the power of substances in their lives with just their own meager strength. The 12-steps teach that such provisions can only come from a higher power.

Alcohol or drug abuse are addictions that normally require spiritual help and intervention for effective control. The psychologically addictive nature of the Red Button experience requires no less supernatural power for meaningful release.

I mentioned mid-life crisis briefly in a previous chapter. A closer look at that middle-aged phenomenon may help put into better perspective the power of lust and our need for victory over it.

The power of the Red Button experience does diminish. In my own life this seemed to begin occurring in my mid-40s (I am in my 50s at the time of this writing). I can recall a sense of panic, even a feeling of disappointment at the gradual loss in the "kick" of the visual sexual experience. That time of transition from powerful sexual arousal to something less powerful, fortunately, did not throw me into too much of a tail spin. The Lord had been leading me and illuminating this area of my thought life for a decade or more and I had read that sexual intensity does diminish with years.

What about those men, though, who reach their middle years and cannot, or do not, put this reduction in the intensity of sexual arousal into its proper place in the aging process? Has the psychological jolt from visual sexual arousal become a significant part of who they are? Is it a large part of how they spend their time, what they discuss with their men friends, what they fantasize about? When the jolt begins moderating, do they become a bit disoriented? Do they begin frantically searching for ways of restoring the sexual kick to that of their younger years? Do they blame this reduced ardor on some fault in their aging wife and search out an affair with a younger woman? Do they seem to take on a somewhat different personality as they search for who they are, apart from the 30-year roller coaster ride of intense visual sexual arousal and release?

My observations of men going through the middle years leads me to suspect that the answer to most of these questions is, "yes." I raise these issues to point out to you younger men that one should not delay in beginning the spiritual process of finding freedom from lust. The earlier in life we can put this powerful force into perspective—the sooner we decide to bring the Lord's healing power into play—the less likely the middle years of our life will find us doing silly, damaging things to ourselves and to our relationships.

Do we want to be healed of the power of lust? That is what Jesus is asking every Christian male above the age of puberty. I believe that our answer to Jesus is easier when we remember that lust is sin, and that the consequences of this sin are much the same as for adultery or for fornication. The helpful instructions of the father (Solomon) to his son in Proverbs 6:20-7:27 speak plainly and frankly about the power of the temptress and about our losses if we give in to her powers. Reread that section of scripture, in light of what I have shared with you about the seductive power of the Red Button experience, and simply substitute in the father's teaching the sin of lust for the actual sex act.

When the father comes to the end of his warnings to his son, he concludes: "All at once he follows her, as an ox goes to the slaughter, or as a stag is caught fast till an arrow pierces its entrails; as a bird rushes into a snare; he does not know that it will cost him his life"(7: 22-23). Solomon draws here the same conclusions James will later include in the first chapter of his New Testament letter. You will recall from our earlier discussion, James taught that surrendering to temptation, following our own desires for that which is tempting us, and acting out the sin, leads to death. In this day of sexually transmitted diseases and of AIDS, death might literally be the case in the indiscriminate engaging in sexual intercourse outside of marriage. The result of consistently giving into the sexual sin of lust is death in a different sense. It results in death to your sense of self value, the choking off of your inclination to enter into guilt-free, intimate relationships with women, or the eventual death of your vitality as a husband, a mate. It may lead to the death of your opportunity to be an example of righteousness to your own children. The author of Proverbs had obviously found some relief from sexual sin. He could give meaningful advice and testimony to his son. Will you be able to do the same for your sons?

Lust is sin. Any follower of Jesus who deliberately chooses to try to hide such a sin from his Lord will find his relationship with God withering. Given enough hardness of heart, death of our discipleship can be the result. My prayer for you young Christian men is that you will not go so far down this trail of addictive mental, sexual sin that you walk away from God, rather than give up your relationship with lust.

God's children want to grow in righteous living, bringing themselves under the will and power of our Lord. Christian men must realize that our sexual thought life is as much a part of God's knowledge of us as are our outward actions. So, we need to recognize our helplessness against the sin of lust and begin to deliberately move toward freedom from its power over us.

Once we face the inevitable and agree that we want to be healed of the power of this sin, we must continue on with implementing the first step: removing those items from our environment that we have intentionally brought in to provide us with regular Red Button experiences. By this I mean the magazines, videos, pictures, etc. We must move on to praying seriously about our use of television. This medium is the entertainment industry's chief route to your Red Button. Sex apparently gets ratings (as does violence). Take stock of what you watch on television and pray for the Lord's illumination of your motive for selecting the shows you watch. I provided our congregation a sign containing David's comments from Psalm 101, suitable for placing on the TV stand. I keep such a sign on my TV at home.

Enough honest soul-searching on your part and you may well come to the surprising discovery I made a number of years ago. Other than the sporting events on TV, much of what you view is with the unconscious hope for visual, sexual arousal. You may even find that you instinctively learn what sections of various commercials and repeated programs will give your Button a gentle push.

It is my contention that few men today will even begin the road to freedom from lust until they have surrendered their television viewing to the Lord. It is easy to see that much of what appears on TV today is designed to be sexually arousing. When we surrender ourselves to those stimuli, rather than surrendering our eyes to the Lord's protection, we are going to be hour by hour participating in sexually lustful experiences.

I find that my television watching has changed significantly, even drastically in the last decade. I have become extremely careful what I permit to come across the TV screen. I select programs which reflect my viewing interest (sports, news, travel), and I am extra careful to avoid any selections that have any potential for sexual content. I never expose myself to the movie offerings that have ratings more mature than PG-13, or comparable content. Is this too naive for an adult television or movie viewer? No! A good plot, a meaningful, enjoyable story intended for adults can be filmed without explicit sexual scenes. The insinuation of sexual relations is sufficient to carry the message!

How about the premium movie channels? Men used to insist that they only bought *Playboy* magazine "to read the articles." Nobody really believed that claim. The same can be said for subscription to premium movie channels and pay-per-view selections. It is my contention that most men pay the premium prices just to get the sexually explicit movies. Examine your own heart on this issue. Check your movie fare over the next month and determine why you choose to watch specific movies. Be honest, in the Lord's presence. I believe such prayerful introspection will change your viewing habits!

Much of what I have said about TV can also be applied to our use of the Internet. Cybersmut is just the latest pornography utility available to American homes. Before the electronic age, one had to leave home to find pornographic materials. Now, just subscribe to cable or an Internet provider and you can have a regular flow of smut delivered right into your living room. Reports are that possibly as much as 80% of web site connections by Internet users is to pornographic sites. I have chosen not to have an Internet connect at home. I use the work-stations at our local public library. I have to get up earlier than the students to get a station, but that is a small price to pay (and I like small prices....I use it also because I am cheap). I know that I could not trust myself with private, home access to an unfiltered Internet service. Whenever this free public connect becomes unreasonable or too difficult in the future for me to schedule, I would consider subscribing to one of the "G-rated" Internet provider services. What keeps you from doing the same? Do you really need the full faucet of junk and porno sites flowing into your home? If you have young boys in the family, do you want to turn them loose with unfiltered access to cybersmut? It is not only a parent's responsibility to help protect adolescent boys from such ready access to electronic pornography, we owe comparable attention to protecting ourselves, as well. I tire of hearing people say, "That is not fit for children to see," while they continue to watch themselves. I have found that a considerable amount of what we believe is not suitable for the eyes of children is also not very healthy for adults! Check the Christian lifestyle magazines and general computer magazines for advertisements by the pre-screened provider services. By changing to such a filtered service you will have taken a good beginning step toward blocking the free flow of Red Button materials into your home.

The next step for us in finding some victories over lust is found in the actions Joseph took in the story recounted in Genesis 39. You will recall that Joseph, one of the sons of Jacob, was sold into slavery by his brothers and eventually found himself in Egypt as household manager for one of the officers of Pharaoh. Verses 6-12 tell of the handsome young Joseph being approached by his master's wife, requesting that he "lie with her." He rejected her sexual requests day after day. One day, apparently out of frustration, "she caught him by his garment, saying 'lie with me.' But he left his garment in her hand, and fled and got out of the house" (verse 12). Joseph did what anyone who truly wishes to resist sin must do: he fled from temptation.

We must develop a habit, a reflex, of fleeing at the first point of temptation. We cannot hang around with the temptation to enjoy a little of the lust pulling on our sleeve. We must learn to recognize that we are being tempted by a situation to just settle back and push the Red Button. Once the danger is recognized we must resist and "flee" from that temptation. In the instances of the temptations to lust, this fleeing normally means that we must put those temptations out of our view, as quickly as we can. We must not take the second look with the intention of just a little sexual arousal. We must change the channel, or turn off the set, or get off the web site, immediately! If we are in a social setting where these actions are not possible, we must close our eyes to the temptation, or divert our gaze somewhere else. I find my movie viewing in the company of others sometimes requires me to look away from the screen at the first evidence that the film maker intends to hit my Button.

If we want to be healed, we must take seriously Peter's warning in his second letter. "Your adversary the devil prowls around like a roaring lion, seeking some one to devour" (5:8). As any reasonably conditioned man would recognize the need to flee from the path of a prowling lion, we need to condition ourselves as well to recognize the danger of temptations to lust. There should be no delay in distancing ourselves from those sources of temptations.

Victory over lust, then, progresses along a path of:

1. Realizing that we need to be healed of this sin.

2.   Taking Jesus' warning that we must take drastic steps to remove from our lives the objects we have put there to push our Red Button.

3.   Fleeing from the source of temptation when we are being tempted to lust. This might include looking away from the source of temptation, closing our eyes to its appeal; or walking away from the scene of the temptation.

4.   Praying for God's protection from this sin, at the very point of the temptation.

This final step in achieving victory over the power of lust may very well be the most important. As Christian disciples we should and do condition ourselves to turn to the Lord with prayers for protection from other sins. If we have problems with destructive anger, we learn to surrender that anger as early as possible to God. We wisely call upon his protective power. The same is true of sins such as covetousness (the overwhelming desire to possess things), an overly critical tongue, or the draw of alcohol or drugs upon those under the addictive power of some substance.

This same sense of needing to be protected from the sin of lust must become a daily reality for those attempting to move toward freedom from this sin. We cannot overcome, in our own strength, the endless temptations to lust which flood our culture. We cannot deal singularly with the frustrations that result from trying to clean up our lust-corrupted thought life. It is only through the Lord's moment-by-moment protective powers that we will find ultimate victory over lust, "For he who is in you is greater than he who is in the world" (1 John 4:4). It is only when we condition ourselves to view all temptations to lust as an attack on us that we then more easily move to seeking God's protection. It is as we flee the attack that we are willing to pray for God's protection and we begin to see healing from this thorn in our flesh. We can then say with Paul, "I can do all things in him who strengthens me" (Philippians 4:13).

Once you have reached this point in your growth toward finding the God-created balance of sexuality in your life, it is a good time to look around for men who are also struggling with this issue. "Accountability" is a popular buzzword in Christian circles these days. Being in relationship with a Christian friend who can help hold you up during times of struggles with lust is essential in this entire process. Habitual lusting is an isolating, lonely preoccupation. Asking a friend to help hold you accountable with this problem can lift you above the isolation.

I have been blessed with a couple of male friends who have not been bashful about talking about their bouts with lustful thoughts and activities. A Saturday morning men's prayer and share group I attended for many years was also open to talking about this sin. These relationships have helped me establish an openness with others regarding this sin in my life. I currently correspond with a Christian friend, and we suggest prayer area needs in our lives each time we write. When I have been struggling with lustful temptations, I have asked him to hold me up in prayer. I am even open to my own congregation from the pulpit about this tap-root sin from my past. I want to be accountable even to the flock I shepherd. I pray, too, that my openness to them will free up some men in the church to approach me about their own struggles.

I know that finding a supportive relationship with another man or a group concerning this sin is difficult. As I have noted repeatedly, I find men generally quite reticent to mention or discuss this topic. It is too personal and embarrassing for many of us. But once you have become serious about gaining some freedom in this area of your discipleship, I encourage you to find a male friend who can help hold you accountable. Such a relationship will help strengthen your intentions to stay on track toward freeing yourself of the Red Button plague.

The number of organizations dedicated to helping men with these sexual problems testifies to the spread of such addictions. One of the oldest and largest of the associations formed to deal with problems of lust and sexual addictions is Sexaholics Anonymous, founded in 1979. As of this writing S.A. has about 8,000 members in over 700 regional groups. These 12-step based support groups assist individuals wishing to stop their sexually self-destructive thinking and behavior such as fantasy, pornography, adultery, masturbation, and incest. You may contact the national office at P.O. Box 111910, Nashville, TN 37222 (E-mail: saico@sa.org) to see if there is a group meeting in your area.

Other such national organizations providing support groups are:

Sex Addicts Anonymous (S.A.A.)
P.O. Box 70949
Houston, TX 77270
(713) 869-4902   (4,500 members in 450 local chapters)

Sex and Love Addicts Anonymous (S.L.A.A.)
          (also known as Augustine Fellowship)
P.O. Box 650010
West Newton, MA 02165-0010
(617) 332-1845   (1,200 groups)

It is also probably a good policy to discuss with your wife, or with your girlfriend if you are not married, your problems with lust. Being able to admit that your thought life sometimes causes you problems in the area of lust, I believe, helps drive this issue out into the open for you. Being able to share such truths with your significant other helps break down some of the guilt that may have been forcing you underground with this secret part of your life. This is a way of verbalizing your problem and of letting some light to begin to shine into this dark area of your thought life.

9

FREEDOM FROM LUST

S in is a broadly destructive force in our lives. The most obvious predicament when we sin is that we find ourselves being put on guard
against God. We hide from him out of fear of punishment. John writes
in his first letter, "There is no fear in love, but perfect love casts out
fear. For fear has to do with punishment, and he who fears is not per-
fected in love (I John 4: 18)." Sin also creates consequences that often
extend into the lives of those around us. Theft and murder leave vic-
tims that experience the sting or devastation of those sins. God even
warns us of these destructive powers of sin in the Ten Commandments: "For I the Lord your God am a jealous God, visiting the iniq-
uity of the fathers upon the children to the third and fourth generation
of those who hate me" (Exodus 20:5).

Sin also retards our spiritual growth. When we sin we not only must
go through the process of repentance and forgiveness to be restored to
our Lord and those around us, but we have also missed an opportunity
for growth. Our growth energies have been dissipated as we have struggled in the cycle of sin-repentance-forgiveness. We might say that sin is
a double step backward in our spiritual and emotional growth. We not
only have to cover the same ground again to reach our former point in
the growth process, but had we not sinned, we would be at a point further along in our growth.

Since lust is sin, we can understand the debilitating nature of lust
and the reason it brings such frustrations into the lives of men. As we
mature and grow in our spiritual and emotional makeup we move
headlong into the reality of mental sexual sin. It defeats us and we

struggle to find some level of relief, only to have it buffet us again. In the chapter on lust and anger we found that this cycle of defeat and relief can bring tremendous frustrations and angers into a man's life. In the life of the Christian man, the path of successful victories over the power of various other sins often ends at the precipice of the Chasm of Lust.

I mentioned earlier that the Lord has brought many freedoms into my life. One of my favorite life scriptures has been John 8:32: "You will know the truth, and the truth will make you free." As an undergraduate at Miami University in Ohio I first read that phrase which was chiseled into the archway above the entrance to the liberal arts building. I embraced that thought, not even knowing at the time that it was from the Bible! I believed the phrase to mean that by throwing off the shackles of restraints that society placed on me, I could live a life of freedom. As an older man I have come to understand it's biblical meaning: a rich, abundant life is achieved through knowing Christ as the Truth of life, and he will set me free from the shackles into which my sinful nature has inevitably placed me.

The Lord has set me free from the dominating power of fear. He has overcome the general power of sin in my life and provided me a wonderful couple of decades free from sin's intimidation and destructive intentions. He has also set me free from the tyranny of lust, and I believe that this has been the greatest victory of all.

Once we find victory over the power of lust we can begin experiencing the freedom of living without its daily control. It is not until we see the sin of lust for what it is, and find God's protection from its power, do we begin realizing what a prisoner we have been to mental sexual sin.

There is a rather crass phrase that is used to describe a guy who finds himself in a bind of some sort. We say that someone or something "has him by the scrotum." Though we normally use this phrase figuratively, it is probably literally true for men caught up in the sensual seductions of today's society. Advertisers, media moguls, large segments of the entertainment industry, and even some women clearly understand that men can be controlled with sexual images. The old adage says, "The way to a man's heart is through his stomach (his appetite)." Today's culture has drafted the adage "The way to a man's attention is through his genitals." We have discovered that route passes first through the eyes of the man. The world says, "Feast your eyes on this!" and we pull up a seat at the feast. The Manipulator says, "Don't you just love the Red Button experience!" and the manipulated just begs for more.

The world has discovered the easiest way to control the lives of men is to fix their attention on the Red Button experience. That should leave us with a realization that men are basically in a power struggle for how we are going to live our lives. But, we find ourselves nearly powerless to resist the hypnotizing strategy of those who find us as willing accomplices in the lustful experience.

The women's liberation movement has attempted in recent decades to set women free from all sorts of issues which the movement's leadership sees as debasing to females. Who will liberate men from their propensity toward following the path of most temptation when it comes to the Red Button experience?

Paul asked a similar question in the letter to the church at Rome. There probably has never been a more insightful expression of one caught in the struggle to be free from the power of sin than Romans 7: 15-25:

> *"I do not understand my own actions. For I do not do what I want, but I do the very thing I hate. Now if I do what I do not want, I agree that the law is good. So then it is no longer I that do it, but sin which dwells within me. For I know that nothing good dwells within me, that is, in my flesh. I can will what is right, but I cannot do it. For I do not do the good I want, but the evil I do not want is what I do. Now if I do what I do not want, it is no longer I that do it, but sin which dwells within me. So I find it to be a law that when I want to do right, evil lies close at hand. For I delight in the law of God, in my inmost self, but I see in my members another law at war with the law of my mind and making me captive to the law of sin which dwells in my*

members. Wretched man that I am! Who will deliver me from this body of death? Thanks be to God through Jesus Christ our Lord! So then, I of myself serve the law of God with my mind, but with my flesh I serve the law of sin."

Paul's lament expresses what most of us have experienced in our struggles against the power of sin. If you reread the above verses from Romans using lust as the sin from which Paul might have been struggling to be free (just as an exercise for you in self understanding) you may find an extra measure of kinship with the First-century apostle. Paul comes to the realization in verse 25 that, "Thanks be to God," he could know freedom from the constant cycle of sin-repentance-forgiveness. Thanks be to our Lord, we too can experience freedom from the intimidation of lustful mental activities. But, that freedom, as with freedom in general, does come with a price for us to pay.

The exchange involves our willingness to give up the small, sensual pleasure of the Red Button lust experience in order to have the incredible universe of riches that God gives us when we are unshackled from sin. We must reach the point where we are willing to forfeit the kick of visual lust in order to embrace the unspeakable peace and beauty in our lives when God truly makes us free.

Jesus' parable of the pearl of great price is one of my favorite illustrations of the truth about the cost of freedom. "Again the kingdom of heaven is like a merchant in search of fine pearls, who, on finding one pearl of great value, went and sold all that he had and bought it (Matthew 13:46)." Some of us within the bounds of our own talents and efforts can amass material successes. We can also experience sensual pleasures, with very little effort. God is calling us to a life so far beyond those minor, incidental belongings and feelings. We must take the step of faith that includes giving up to him what little we have experienced on our own in order that he can provide us with unimaginable blessings in life.

The story is told of a wealthy family driving down to Florida for a vacation, riding comfortably in their luxury car. The husband and wife were in the front seat of the plush automobile and their two children (who enjoyed generous allowances) and their nanny were dozing in the rear seat. Seeking a short break from the interstate highway in the hills of Tennessee, the father decided to meander across a short stretch of state road. Just a few minutes along the route the dad saw a small shack up ahead which was still smoldering from a very recent fire. The gentle falling rain had put out some of the flames, but the charred remains were adding a gray smoke to the dark afternoon sky.

A few hundred feet ahead the driver saw a woman and two children walking along the berm. The mother's back was arched against the chilling rain while she kept a firm grasp on the children's hands. He drove up, stopped and pushed the button to roll down his wife's window. "We saw a burning house back there. Was anyone hurt?" he shouted past his wife out the open window.

"It's our place, and we're OK" the young mother sadly replied. "We're on our way up the road to a friend's place."

The Christian businessman asked if the three would care to have a lift to their destination, and a chance to get out of the rain. "No, that's OK, it's not too much farther, and we don't want to get your car all messed up," the woman said.

"Well, I hate to see anyone burned out of their home. Let me help you a little," he said, reaching a $50 bill past his wife, out the window. "We can spare it!"

The woman was hesitant at first, not knowing what to make of these people in the beautiful car. "Go ahead, take it! We insist," the husband offered once again.

"OK, that's really nice of you. We can sure use some extra money, cause we don't have no insurance on our place or our stuff." She reached inside the passenger window and took the money. "And God bless you and your family," the man smiled a farewell as he began to ease back onto the highway.

The family had driven only a short distance before the man's conscience began bothering him. "Your family has so much and that woman and her children have lost everything. The money that your family will spend on this one vacation alone would go a long way toward rebuilding much of that small shack. God may have additional ways of caring for that woman, but you certainly can do more than what you've done." His thoughts convicted. He brought the car to an abrupt stop, jerking all the passengers wide awake.

Pulling to the side of the road he took off his golf hat and said to the others in the car, "Quick, put all your cash in my hat!" The startled wife, children and baby-sitter started to protest, but realized he was serious. Everyone, including the driver, tossed all their ready vacation cash into the hat. The man looked it over quickly and found that the hasty collection amount to nearly $400. He spun the car around and drove back toward the spot where they had last seen the fire victims walking.

He shortly spotted the trio, still on their rainy trek. Once again, pulling along side, he opened the passenger window. "We're back again!" he shouted across to her. Before the woman could respond he said, "I would like that $50 back we gave you."

The woman was nearly speechless with anger, hardly believing what he had just requested. She probably thought, "This has got to be the cruelest person and the meanest trick I have ever seen!" In disgust the woman wadded up the bill in her palm and tossed it into the passenger's lap.

The husband snatched up the wad, added it to the heap of cash in this golf hat and held it out to the woman. "Here, you needed more than I gave you before. Please just keep this, hat and all!"

The startled, embarrassed woman started to protest. Without another word, the window closed in front of her and the car pulled away.

The mother in this touching story was faced at a moment in time with the decision that we all must make. Are we willing to give up what little we have gained for the moment, in order to receive the abundance that God truly wants us to have? Those who are at the threshold of freedom from lust must be willing to surrender what little sensual pleasure that visual, sexual arousal has to offer. We then can begin receiving the immeasurable blessings of peace, productivity, deepened relationships, stronger marriages, and more authentic Christian witness that God has waiting for us. "Give, and it will be given to you; good measure, pressed down, shaken together, running over, will be put into your lap" (Luke 6:38).

It is as if the most compelling sensual pleasure that God has given us to experience in life is ultimately denied us. But our Creator is telling us that it is only through our surrender of that level of sensuality that we can experience the more abundant life and pleasures that he has intended for us.

I have known the slavery of sexual lust. I have also known the blessings of freedom from that incessant plague on the lives of men. My witness and testimony to you is that the freedom is far better. The blessings of God's riches beyond this most base of activities of men are so far greater that it is worth the small price to be paid. My prayer at this moment is that none of you men reading this book will settle for the darkness and captivity of the habits of sexual lust in your life. May you persevere until God has provided you the rich life available to those who find freedom from the power of lust.

10

GOD'S INTENTIONS FOR OUR SEXUAL SATISFACTION

I opened this book with the statement "It would appear that God intends that most men should marry." We come now to a further discussion of what our Creator seems to have in mind for fulfilling the sexuality that He has placed within us men.

It is important to note here that, at this point in the process, most of you have not yet reached freedom from lust. For Christian single men this might well be the most important victory in their struggles with sexuality. If the Lord has led them into the single life, or they find themselves in that situation through factors beyond their control, freedom for them is at hand. Being free from the unfulfilling treachery of sexual lust may well be the foundation for much of the mental peace they will enjoy in life. The single male finds freedom and peace by ridding his life of this plague.

For most of us, however, it would appear that the Lord has prepared us to be in sexual relations within the arrangement of marriage. Finding mutual sexual satisfaction in marriage, I believe, requires the husband to be free from constant intimidation by the world as it reaches for his Red Button. It also requires dedicating himself to God's plan for him as a husband.

There is a real spiritual danger in trying to clean up a sin without preparing to replace it with something of substance. Nature may abhor a vacuum, but Satan seems to love them. Jesus tells of what happens when we take only the preliminary step of having our lives cleansed of sin, but do not then fill that clean, empty void with something of substance. Luke 11: 24-25:

> *"When the unclean spirit has gone out of a man, he passes through waterless places seeking rest,; and finding none he says, 'I will return to my house from which I came.' And when he comes he finds it swept and put in order. Then he goes and brings seven other spirits more evil than himself, and they enter and dwell there; and the last state becomes worse than the first."*

Jesus' parable speaks to both the scientific principle and the spiritual principle of displacement. When water is poured into a glass, it does not simply fill the glass, it displaces the air that was contained in the glass before we began pouring. Where the water comes in, the air can no longer remain, because it has been displaced.

A more meaningful illustration of this is found in the two building blocks of the universe: light and dark. Darkness is the background against which all the good things of the universe are played out. That is true even of the darkness near us. Your bedroom may be totally dark when you prepare to enter it at night. When you click the light switch, the room is filled with light. What happened to the darkness? Has it been destroyed or has it merely been displaced? Turn the switch off and you will find out. The darkness returns. It would be futile to try to just get rid of the darkness with some handy appliance, like a darkness vacuum. It can not be gathered up and destroyed. It can only be displaced by the energy of the light, but when that energy is no longer in place, the darkness can return.

Sin is darkness. Sin is the background against which all the good things of humanity are played out. Sin cannot be destroyed as much as it can be displayed by spiritual light. We know from scripture that Jesus is "the Light of the world." Wherever Jesus is brought in, the sin will be displaced. To try to simply do away with sin leads to frustration and failure. To surrender ourselves to Jesus and his light provides the spiritual energy to displace the sin with something better and more powerful.

Victory over lust and eventual freedom from its overwhelming power provides us the foundation. Freedom is not complete until the void left by our sin is filled. The final step is taking our newly uncluttered heart, mind and spirit and filling our marriage relationship with what our Lord apparently intended: unconditional love and surrender to each other's needs. Our Christian marriage vows commit us to establishing our marriage partner as that which must fill that void. Our wife must become the most important human being in our life; parents, brothers or sisters, close friends, and future children not withstanding.

Let's take a look at how God provides for the husband who is being healed of the sin of lust. The Lord's commission to the husband is quite clear and powerful. Ephesians 5: 25-33 reads:

> *"Husbands, love your wives, as Christ loved the church and gave himself up for her, that he might sanctify her, having cleansed her by the washing of water with the word, that he might present the church to himself in splendor, without spot or wrinkle or any such thing, that she might be holy and without blemish. Even so husbands should love their wives as their own bodies. He who loves his wife loves himself. For no man ever hates his own flesh, but nourishes and cherishes it, as Christ does the church, because we are members of his body. 'For this reason a man shall leave his father and mother and be joined to his wife, and the two shall become one.' This is a great mystery, and I take it to mean Christ and the church; however, let each one of you love his wife as himself, and let the wife see that she respects her husband."*

Husbands, this is the quality of relationship that the Lord wants us free to participate in with our wives. This is the level of selfless, unconditional love that He intends for us when we say, "I do" at the marriage altar. Our God is saying to us, "Husbands, I probably will not ask you to go to the cross for your wife, but I ask you to commit yourself to her the way Jesus committed himself to death to self on the tree." If we are going to have any insights into what Jesus' death means, those revelations will probably come to us husbands through our life commitment to our wife.

What do we men give up to begin married life? What are the typical sacrifices that men make in order to help a marriage work? Unencumbered time with old friends would be one sacrifice. If love equals time in the building of relationships (and it certainly does) the strength of our marriage bonds may well develop in direct proportion to the hours we are willing to commit to our wife and their daily needs.

Another sacrifice might be the amount of time we spend in the hobbies we developed as young people: sports, tinkering with cars, wood working, computers, and the like. Giving of ourselves to new, mutually satisfying activities with our wives will build our relationship with her as little else can. Yes, this might even mean learning to pretend to enjoy shopping, even on a day when a crucial tournament game is to be on television!

But, what does all of this have to do with our sexuality? I have defined the two areas of male sexuality as the visual, sexual arousal experience (The Red Button experience) and actual physical, relational sex with a partner. A man who has grown up with a visual, sexual addiction must learn to replace that vicarious sex with a healthy, mutually fulfilling experience of intimacy and sex with his wife. This displacement of the Red Button habit is complete when this is more fully understood.

To begin with, most men need a better understanding of intimacy. Christian psychologists DeLoss and Ruby Friesen in their book *Counseling and Marriage* (Word Publishing, 1989) include a helpful chart they call the "sexual ladder." I often use this chart in premarital and in marital counseling. The illustration shows the progression of a healthy man/woman relationship, beginning with the progression of those activities which characterize a growing friendship: looking at each other; small talk; working on a project; going for a walk; sharing plans;

touching while talking; laughing together; sharing dreams; walking arm in arm.

These activities of growing intimacy grow into evidences of affection for each other: a gentle hug; saying "I love you;" a lingering kiss; a full body embrace; nonbreast/nongenital touch. Friesens' "ladder" (which I like to call the "intimacy ladder") then moves into sexual relations: French kissing; fondling the breasts; genital caressing; and sexual intercourse.

This gradual growth from friend, to intimate, to spouse and lover is the traditional steps of what was once known as "courting." The slow, planned process of growing intimacy, leading to marriage and sexual relations has been crushed in our age of casual sex, "one night stands" and fever-pitch arousal from pornography. Men who are conditioned to quick, visual sexual arousal and some quick, easy way of relieving those tensions (either with a woman or without) are missing the essence of sex the way God designed and intended it. They have settled for a quick hot dog at the food cart when our Creator has set a full table of roast beef, vegetables, breads, and desserts to please our sexual palates. Our age of instant everything is quickly loosing the most wonderful gift that God has given us: deep, rich, rewarding intimacy and sexual fulfillment between husband and wife.

I can recall a time shortly after we were married that I was "reading" an adult magazine in my wife's presence. She observed, with no little bit of disgust in her voice, "I thought when you were married that you wouldn't need those types of magazines any more." My own reaction was that I did not need those magazines, I just found them interesting. My wife had hit the nail right on the head, though. Not only had I developed the habit of mental sexual lust, but my habit had begun making her feel a bit uneasy. Her disdain for my "reading" activities also demonstrated a bit of jealousy, even anxiety, on her part as my spouse. Women, don't be afraid to say something similar to this to your husband, if you see him spending time with pornography. We husbands need to hear that our use of such materials intimidate and anger you.

Just as old friends and old hobbies can become competition for the time it takes to begin building strong marriage relationships, mental sexual lust can, and does, undermine the attitude we need as new husbands. If we are going to construct a marriage of mutually satisfying intimacy and sexual relations, the competition from sexually explicit materials must go. Breaking free from such habits shows a maturity in us as husbands and builds trust and confidence in our wives.

When my wife was surprised that I still "needed" those magazines, it was the first time anyone had ever pointed out to me that I probably had a certain dependency on the Red Button experience for my sexuality. I suspect that many of you men, if you take time to analyze your non-relational sexual activities, will also recognize such a dependency within yourselves.

But the Lord is calling us to surrender that psychological dependency, no less than if we were dependent on an illegal substance, rather than upon controlled and practiced hormone rushes. I believe He calls us to move to this higher level in our relationship with our wives. He defines that dependency on the Red Button experience as a sin against him and against our wife. He has called us to give ourselves sexually to only one woman, either physically or mentally. Our God is calling all Christian husbands to find their sexual satisfaction and pleasure, both physical and mental pleasure, in just one woman alone: our wife.

I recall a story which frames this need for husbands to ultimately commit at this level. A man told of a farm he drove past in the country. Printed on the barn was the name of that spread: "Done Lookin'." The storyteller suggested that the owner of that farm must have checked out several places before he finally settled down on those acres. That is also what our God requires of us when we finally settle into marriage. He expects us, men and women alike, to be "done lookin'." The Bible indicates that it is the Lord's intention that we commit our energy, time, mind and body to providing for the needs of our spouse. He expects us to end our sexual searching and to settle those interests in no one other than our spouse.

Wow, what a tall order in this age of home delivery of smut! I suspect that this oneness has been a difficult requirement from the very beginning of man-woman relations, once Adam and Eve's offspring began encountering the rest of the second generation beyond the Garden. Mankind has probably always been tempted to look and touch beyond the spouse at home, just to sample the grass on the other side of the fence. The real point of frustration comes for us men when we realize through Christ's teachings that we are asked to give up the mental sexual sins which also violate our marriage. This is a crucial point in our lives as faithful, growing husbands. It is not until we give up the mental sexual sins, not until we are ready to become dependent upon our wives for all our sexual relations (both mental and physical) that we are on the threshold of finding sexual satisfaction in our lives.

Freedom from lust puts us at the place where we can begin to experience what our Creator had in store for us when he designed us sexually: mutual satisfaction and gratification within our marriage relationship. The fervent question of many of you, looking for the first time at going "cold turkey" without your active sexual fantasy lives, probably is, "Does this really work?" I would like to try to convince you that it does.

When we are finally able to turn our attention to the needs of our wives, we find that we really do not understand what they need. If we have been committed to a life involving active Red Button pushing, our attention has been too long diverted from the needs of our wife to our own selfish wants. Selfish sex has been sinful sex. "Christian sex" will lead us to a genuine desire to meet our wife's needs. That begins with turning our attention to the question: what it is that makes women tick anyhow? What do they really need from us?

Answering that question brings me to a rather difficult point of discussion, since I have never been a woman. I suspect that my wife, or your wife, could better fill in this section. There are excellent books on this subject, and I recommend that each of you husbands spend some time with such a volume. One excellent one is James Dobson's *What Wives Wish Their Husbands Knew About Women* (which goes well beyond issues of intimacy). At this writing the Dobson book is available in both print and audio formats.

I recall a session I attended a few years ago conducted by a wonderful saint named Mary Webster. Mary took the men aside at a weekend marriage retreat and tried to help us understand the most basic needs of women. She began by stating that the key to understanding women is realizing that every woman wants to be "possessed" by a man…that she wants to be the very special, singularly most important person in some man's life. She wants to be literally at the center of his attention…the one he cannot live without or cannot stop thinking about. She wants to know that she is uniquely his, and that there is not, and will not be another woman for him. In short, she wants to know that she is capable of making someone a one-woman man. A portion of her peace and security in life rests on achieving this special place in one man's life.

If Mary Webster was right about women's emotional needs (and subsequent years of experience convince me she was not far off the mark), her words speak volumes for us in our relationship with our wives. We can add this insight to the description of the intimacy and sexual needs of women discussed in an earlier chapter, and we get this kind of profile for the woman to whom we are married:

• She is most secure and satisfied when she is the only woman in her husband's life.

• She is most emotionally and psychologically fulfilled when he provides her with regular times of intimacy, romance, and touching, which sometimes lead to an unhurried time of sexual relations.

This is not to insinuate that women do not need sex in their lives, or that most do not find any real pleasure in the sex act. There are many times in a marriage when the wife may instigate a time of sexual relations and may even find the husband not in the mood for such activity. This is to say, however, that the sexual needs of men and women are distinctly different. Recognizing these differences is an essential part of our understanding of women. And, one of the critical differences is the importance she places on the one-to-one commitment bond which cradles the female's needs.

It is easy to see that a husband who has been committed to regular schedules of mental sexual lust with other women, or with their images, is going to miss the mark when it comes to both his wife's emotional and physical needs. He is going to be fairly disinterested in her at times, in favor of his mental sex life. If he is obvious about his interest in the sexual images of other women, this will threaten his wife's place as the center of his attention. If he sneaks around with such activities, she will probably be even more threatened, realizing that her husband's interest in "these other women" is something he is trying to hide, and something of which he is ashamed. The Red Button life will tend to arouse him quickly and intensely, tending him toward rather poor preparation for the type of unhurried and deliberate sexual intimacy that a women desires. He will pay little attention to her need for caressing, touching, romancing…all that provides meaning in the sex act for his wife.

So, on balance, those of us men who come into our marriage relationship with the destructive habits of an active life with the Red Button are like landscapers who approach an undeveloped lawn not with rakes, rollers and aerators, but with backhoes and road graders. He simply is going to smash and destroy the landscape, rather than cultivate and develop it. To mix my metaphors, the highly and deliberately aroused husband becomes the bull in the china shop of his wife's romance. Repairing the damage done by a husband addicted to pornography can be difficult and long term.

You might ask, though, how about us men? Don't husbands have needs, too? If we cannot have our videos, magazines and girl watching, what good is life! If we have been conditioned to find our most potent psychological kick from the Red Button, what can our life amount to without those calculated jolts? Those still under the power of the sin of lust are blinded by Satan into not being able to see what all the Lord has in store for them in their relationships. They are settling for just the whipped cream when the Lord has intended that their lives be blessed with the entire sundae.

What do men need? After more than a half-century of life and over 30 years of marriage, I think I am about ready to answer this perplexing question. The Bible's earliest Genesis 2:18 record of God's observations about the male touches on our most basic need: "Then the Lord God said, 'It is not good that the man should be alone; I will make him a helper fit for him'" (Genesis 2:18). One of our most basic needs as men is companionship. If I were to ask a group of men (of mixed ages) what they most need in life, many would put sex near the top of the list. It is clear to me, however, that men, as they age and get a bit wiser, find that companionship with a good woman becomes increasingly important. In fact, it would appear to me that both the Bible and life experiences would put that need, over the lifetime of a man, at the top of our needs. I believe it to be even more basic than sex. The interesting thing is that women know this all along. It just takes us men a number of years and a succession of failings in our relationships to get the message…to put it all in balance.

We begin in our childhood making friends with the guys in the neighborhood and at school. We build strong, lasting bonds with those guys on through junior high and high school. Some of us also add close friendships and bonds with guys we meet at college or in the military. It is difficult to imagine what life would have been like for us had we not had those close, male companions throughout our early lives as boys and young men.

As we mature, friendships normally begin forming with girls, as well. As we begin dating regularly, these boy/girl relationships even begin competing with our friendship with the guys. There is something natural and biological that keeps us growing in interest in our girl friends. Eventually many of us break away from the daily, close ties with family members and male friends to join into marriage with one of these special, female companions. The wife becomes the most immediate, present, available and special friend we are going to have in our lifetime, beginning on that wedding day.

I believe we can see that men have a significant need, even a basic, God-created need for companionship, when we see how ineffective many men are at living alone and isolated. I have had several male friends over the years who did not marry and lived in small apartments apart from much regular social contact. These friends were not singles with active social lives, but ones living apart. Though some seemed to become reasonably acclimated to their rather lonely lives, in comparison, their existences have seemed rather thin, unproductive and lonely when seen alongside the many full, rich lives of the happily married men I have numbered among my friends.

The second century Roman emperor and Stoic philosopher Marcus Aurelius wrote in his *Meditations* ((Penguin Books, 1964, p. 85), "For it has been made clear long ago that fellowship is the purpose behind our creation."

There is also the general observation that many have made that women not only seem to get along better living by themselves, but they tend to make it through widowhood more successfully than do men when they lose their wives. Men do not seem to grow and produce, nor do they seem as fulfilled alone and isolated, as they do when they have an active life companion. My testimony, and that of so many other middle-aged men, is that our need for companionship becomes clearer to us as the years go by. As we reach those years when the sex drive is not as intense and confusing, our more basic, underlying need for the close companionship of our wife is daily unveiled. I need and appreciate the time I spend with my wife today more than in our earlier days of marriage. I only wish that I could have realized this earlier in life, so that I could have made our first years of marriage as rich as these middle years have been. Had I found freedom from lust earlier, I suspect that might have occurred. Our fulfillment in rich relationship, companionship, rests just below the surface of the selfish aspects of our sex drives.

If a man over-values sex as his greatest need during the early years, lost opportunities in building rich, deep relationships with a woman will not be the only blight on his life. He may also tend toward being one who sets off in search of lost sexual drives in their his middle years. Men who panic at the early signs of diminishing sex drive and bolt from their marriage with "the wife of their youth" are depriving themselves of the richest, most satisfying, most basic experience of their years on earth: the years of love and companionship after the children are raised. This loss of fulfillment is one of the truly tragic aspects of our era of easy and foolish divorces.

So, we men are created to need companionship. What else do we need? One of the next things we discover about God's creative intents is in his first commandment: "Be fruitful and multiply (populate the earth)" (Genesis 1:28). This commandment was discussed in an earlier chapter, but is it worth repeating here. It is obvious, in all that is within us guys, our Lord wanted to guarantee that we men got this message. He has created the intense, demanding, sometimes nearly overwhelming sex urges in us that keep our attention clearly focused on his first request for us. Underneath that intense sexual desire, however, is the same little boy who needed someone to play ball with in the first grade, who wanted someone to go to the junior high football game with, who later hoped someone would come by to help him have fun changing the plugs on his first car in high school, and still later wanted that special girl to sit close beside him all evening on the couch at the fraternity party.

My message to you young men is that we can do without a little of the sex that we desire, without hurting us very much. I have heard it said that no man ever died from lack of sex, and I supposed that is essentially true. We do seem to die a slow death, however, when we underestimate our need for healthy relationship and companionship with a women.

I would characterize our needs as husbands, then, as needing the loving, caring attention of our wives, and needing her to recognize that our package as men includes a rather regular release from our natural sexual urges. But, your wife and you both need to clearly understand that you, husband, complicate and blur these two priorities if you permit yourself to be lured into a life of Red Button pushing.

Given the needs I have earlier described for the wife and the needs of men just addressed, how can our God ever possibly hope to have us find mutual satisfaction? Has he created us so opposite in needs that we are doomed to failure in our relationship from the start?

I am writing this book, in part, because I believe that one of the most caustic and damaging elements today that eats away at the mutual satisfaction of husbands and wives is the mental sexual sins of husbands. In past generations, before the advent of television, pornographic magazines, sexually explicit movies and videos, and cybersmut, the actual act of adultery might have been the most prevalent problem in marital growth and harmony. The Red Button experience is so easy and so prevalent today, however, that lust may well be approaching the number-one ranking as killer of marriages. It can be such a quiet, private killer that neither the husband nor wife may early recognize the symptoms of the venom at work.

Once a husband begins seeing the damage lust is doing and moves on to finding freedom from the power of this sin, the process of really satisfying the needs of man and wife can begin. It is possible for physical/relational sex to become more important in a husband's life than the Red Button experience once the overwhelming power of visual sexual arousal has been defeated. God has intended us to meet the needs of our wives, emotionally and sexually, and in so doing, our needs are also met.

Paul summarizes the physical aspect of marriage so well in I Corinthians 7: 1-5:

"Now concerning the matters about which you wrote. It is well for a man not to touch a woman. But because of the temptation to immorality, each man should have his own wife and each woman her own husband. The husband should give to his wife her conjugal rights, and likewise the wife to her husband. For the wife does not rule over her own body, but the husband does; likewise the husband does not rule over his own body, but the wife does. Do not refuse one another except perhaps by agreement for a season, that you may devote yourselves to prayer; but then come together again, lest Satan tempt you through lack of self-control."

The teaching here shows that the husband and wife should seek to be mutually committed to meeting the physical needs of the other. Their bodies have been provided them by the Lord, in part, to be used in loving service in satisfying the physical and emotional needs of their marriage partner. I especially appreciate that Paul has mentioned the responsibility of the husband first. I believe the Lord's system requires the husband to take the lead in meeting the needs of his wife.

To review part of Paul's letter to the Ephesians:

"Husbands, love your wives, as Christ loved the church and gave himself up for her, that he might sanctify her, having cleansed her by the washing of water with the word, that he might present the church to himself in splendor, without spot or wrinkle or any such thing, that she might be holy and without blemish. Even so husbands should love their wives as their own bodies. He who loves his wife loves himself" (5:25-28).

The catalyst in the successful husband-wife relationship should be the sacrificial love of the husband, as he provides for the needs of his wife. He should approach this responsibility by making the same types of careful preparations he might take in caring for his own body. The husband who is experiencing new freedom from the power of lust should approach the loving care of his wife's needs with the same calculating zeal he once used to secure materials for pushing his Red Button.

A rather common fault of husbands would appear to be that we approach our sexual relations with our wives as a means of meeting our own sexual needs, with little or no regard for hers. This is probably especially true of a husband who is actively involved with visual sexual arousal, since his heightened sexual tensions will prowl the house like a young lion looking for prey. With the Red Button fully depressed, a husband is not in a very self-sacrificing frame of mind.

So, husbands, we should begin our time of freedom from the demands of our Red Button by consciously working with our wife's need for attention, time, intimacy, and romance. We should deliberately plan and arrange many of those occasions when such attentions do lead to sexual activity. When we reach this point of sexual maturity, we have come a long way from that husband who was simply expecting his wife to regularly help him release the sexual tensions he had built up by using images in magazines or on a screen.

The first benefit we can begin noticing from our reaching out, deliberately and consciously, to romance our wives is that we begin to rather like it. Somehow it feels right, even if it does not in any way replicate the Red Button experience. A wife will normally begin to respond positively to such honest attention. A man should usually see a reduction of tensions in his relationship with his wife, and should eventually see a reduction of sexual frustrations and tensions in himself. To repeat an earlier point, a reduction in the amount of attention we pay to sexual arousal is good for us. It permits these energies to be used in other creative ways. Diminished sex drive can be good and healthy, if we have artificially built up those drives.

At this first level of freedom, you begin realizing that you have been shooting yourself in the foot sexually with the constant Red Button activities. If you are smart, you will start to see that much of the sexual frustration you have been living with was self-induced, and not easily or reasonably released. One who is serious about eliminating Red Button activities should begin seeing his anger level go down a notch, as well.

Am I saying, then, that the husband who is experiencing freedom from the burden of lust might be on the right track toward being a more attentive and thoughtful husband? Right on! One discovery accompanying freedom from lust is just how time-consuming a habit of lust can be! Freed from this burden, he can begin spending more time planning ways of supporting and helping with the chores his wife faces, both within and outside the home. He should then begin planning times when he and his wife can be alone, as a couple: meals out on a weekend, an evening of watching a video (one his wife chooses....not one of those sexually explicit ones from his past). The best time for young couples can be those moments alone on the couch after the kids have gone to bed, or a quick lunch together just so you can let her know you care how her day has been going.

The husband who is free from the demands of his Red button, and who is beginning to commit himself to serving his wife in these ways, is now beginning to meet her most basic need: to be the most important person (especially the most important woman) in his life. He is now building his marriage along the lines the Lord has intended.

Back to one of our key considerations. What does he get out of all this? He has given up the most powerful psychological jolt he can experience with the surrender of the Red Button to his Creator. What does God have in store for meeting his needs? First, it is important to note that Paul's teaching in his letter to the Ephesians indicated that a husband's love should be of the quality of sacrifice that Jesus showed in giving himself up for the church. So, our love, devotion and energies toward our wife should be with no deliberate intent for rewards in the marriage relationship. She is the most important person on the face of the earth to us now, and our highest level of satisfaction in life may well come from providing for her in every way possible.

There is also a most unexpected benefit for the husband which can result from healthy, growing physical/relational sex with his wife. Over time, visual sexual arousal typically dulls a man to the deep physical pleasures of touch. When a man is surrendered to sexual arousal and satisfaction being contained within the physical act with his wife, a rich new pleasure level can be reached. The slow, touch arousal as part of a giving, unselfish sex act can lead to levels of sexual satisfaction unattainable from over stimulated, hurried sex. "Christian sex" (unselfish sex) is more satisfying than selfish sex. The sexual experience for men who have learned to surrender to slow arousal through touching is far superior to the over-cooked, visually aroused experience.

The foundation the husband is now building in his marriage is the platform on which a lifetime of companionship can grow. He has begun providing for her in a way that is helping her become his best friend, and she is less likely to stray beyond the marriage to find another to meet her needs. He is working on that most basic, God-created need in both sexes: companionship. Long after the sexual drive in the husband has begun moderating, his efforts toward solidifying his wife-as-best-friend will begin paying dividends in companionship.

In addition to being on our way toward making our wife the most significant person in our life, we derive an additional benefit from these loving attentions paid her. Fortunately our Creator has also given to women a genuine need for occasional release of physical and sexual tensions. Most wives are willing to honor the idea Paul expressed in chapter seven of First Corinthians. They recognize their husband's need for sexual relations. Equally important, they have a general desire and need as well for the wonderful gift our Creator has given us in the act of coming together sexually and the unparalleled release we get in that act. The bonus for the wife of a man who is no longer living under the power of the Red Button is that she is now married to a guy who really seems to care about her sexual needs. He is not just using her for his own benefit and release of tensions. Her husband seems to have a new sense of wanting to make the sex act an integral part of their continuing love for each other. In all of these ways sex becomes better for both partners.

The increased satisfaction she will now draw from the sex act will help her increase her own interest in intercourse as the outcome of intimacy. The man who is freed from the power of lust is liberated to make his wife more sexually fulfilled. The ultimate payoff for him is that he becomes more sexually fulfilled as well: greater satisfaction from the sex act and more interest in sexual frequency from his wife.

In the two realms of male sexuality the husband can now discover that the best sex, by far, is relational sex, when it is done well. Visual sexual arousal for him used to be a quick sexual high, but ultimately a frustrating experience. It seldom led to the sex act with his wife being part of a desire to meet her sexual needs. It was often accompanied by guilt (God's assigned emotion for combating sin). But now, with his freedom from that lust syndrome, he can continue his efforts at meeting his wife's needs right into the bedroom.

So, we husbands get best friends and companions in the person of our wives, and we begin finding some true sexual satisfaction. You will recall that Paul cautioned in First Corinthians that we humans, both men and women, tend toward sexual temptation and immorality. Therefore, he observed, most of us are probably best served by having a marriage partner. Marriage itself does lay the foundation for sexual satisfaction for men. It certainly does not guarantee sexual satisfaction for husbands, but it typically sets up the conditions under which a proper, productive exercise of our sexuality may well lead to reasonable sexual fulfillment and peace for us.

As men under the power of the Red Button we literally hungered for visual sexual arousal. Jesus has something else in mind for us, as seem in his teaching in the Sermon on the Mount: "Blessed are those who hunger and thirst for righteousness, for they shall be satisfied" (Matthew 5:6). What brings us satisfaction in life? Regular doses of porno or cybersmut? Hardly! That brings frustration. What brings us fulfillment is living out our days and our designs in the right way ("righteousness" literally means "full of rightness")…the way our Creator has intended us to live. When we are right with the Lord, we are righteous, or full of rightness.

This is true in life generally, and it is true when it comes to the sexuality of men. When we are calling on God's protection from the power of lust, and when we are deliberately and actively seeking the best for our wives spiritually, physically, emotionally and sexually, we are living our lives as husbands in the righteous way. We are also positioning ourselves for the greatest sexual satisfaction that we can expect from life. We are freed from the frustrating burdens of lust. This is a contentment that only one who has known such oppression can appreciate. We are building our skills and prowess in the realm of physical/relational sex with our spouses. This is the realm of male sexuality where satisfaction is to be achieved.

Sexuality in men has possibly the highest potential for creating or for destroying those around us. Probably no other aspect of our life holds more promise for bringing positive results to our days on earth. Those results include: a wife who loves and respects us and wishes to be our intimate mate; new human beings brought into the world as a result of this loving intimacy; and, having the strongest psychological prompting we experience in life being channeled toward the edification of those around us.

But, male sexuality also holds possibly the highest potential for destroying our own life and the lives of those within our reach. Those outcomes may include: debilitating, self-indulgent lust; abuse of females around us through rape, incest or child molestation (as an inappropriate expression of the frustrations brought on by such lust); and wives who are emotionally and sexually alone in their marriages due to husbands who permit their sexuality to become destructive, rather than creative and righteous.

11

LOVE OR LUST?

I have heard it said that Mark Twain once observed (I believe the quote is also variously assigned to Mae West.): "I have been poor and I have been rich, and rich is better." My testimony to you within this book has been that I have lived under the power of destructive lust and I have known freedom from lust. Freedom is better.

As I look back over my years growing up in the 1950s and compare the temptations in the 50s and 60s to those on young males today, I can clearly see the startling increase in sexual temptations. From those days during the Great Depression when my brother and dad alternately found and hid the "girlie magazine" in the outbuildings on the farm, to these days of pornography as a utility, funneled right into the living room through the TV and the computer, it is clear that open season has been declared on the Red Button of all American men. I now realize that I have literally dodged a bullet by arriving when I have at a point of productive marriage and family. The struggle against addiction to sexually explicit materials is not getting any easier for boys and men. It is clearly getting more difficult.

Beginning with my generation, and continuing particularly into the generation of my sons and my grandsons, we can see ourselves as pioneers in a hideous social experiment. We have been placed in a culture of graphic, sexually exciting images plastered everywhere and anywhere that the human eye can possibly fall. We are the pioneering generations of men. We must determine if the human male, as a sexual being, can function in a healthy and productive way when his attention is daily enticed by efforts to arouse him sexually: standing in line at the supermarket, watching a ball game on TV, reading a news magazine, taking a spin in the boat or a walk on the beach. The big question facing the men of our generations is, will our lives ultimately achieve love or lust?

Our Lord God Creator has ordained that love is to be the achievement of our lives. Jesus said the greatest commandment is "You shall love the Lord your God with all your heart, and with all your soul and with all your mind...(and)...you shall love your neighbor as yourself" (Matthew 22:37-39). Each generation seems to rediscover the most basic of all biblical truths: "It's love that makes the world go 'round." The type of achievements that will characterize each of our lives as sons, boy friends, husbands and fathers will depend upon how well we learn to love our Lord and to love those he has entrusted to us in relationships. If we are to build creative, successful lives it is because we will have learned that maturity means the loving, sacrificial giving of ourselves to those around us. This quality of life is what the German theologian Detroit Bonhoeffer called, being "a man for others."

Love does not grow and prosper in a life that is committed to sinful activities. Sin turns one's interest and attention back upon one's self. The sinful self tends to block out both the light and the lessons awaiting that person if he were not grounded in sin. Lust is sin. Lust captures the attention of the young mind and holds it captive to images which feed self-satisfaction and self-gratification. Lust is the base, self-conscious level of male sexuality. It is entry-level sex that, if not recognized for what it is, can lead that growing mind to turning in upon its own sexual impulses. Lust is sexual experience and expression that recognizes only the basest needs of a man. A healthy participation in life-building relationships requires that we men work beyond the base level of lust.

The social and spiritual leaders of tomorrow are going to be those men who are able to find freedom from the destructive power of lust. Sexual promiscuity has been part of our society since the very beginning of mankind. In recent years, stories of political leaders who have had sexual flings with staff members or starlets are regular fare in the media. The social and political calamities of the Bill Clinton administration were a harbinger of the destruction that can hound future leaders who give into sexual selfishness. Similar tales about church leaders who have run off with secretaries or have been discovered in sexual misconduct have become nearly as common as those of political leaders. The entertainment industry does not have such scandals. We seem to hold Hollywood to a different standard. We simply expect actors and actresses to have open and unashamed affairs. Faithful marriages in that industry seem to be as scarce as calorie charts at a church potluck.

Open sexual misconduct has plagued every generation. It is our coming generations of men and women, however, who will have to find the strength to overcome the devastating effects of men gone into emotional hiding under the power of mental sexual sin. As Christ indicated that people would be divided into two groups at the time of judgment (sheep and goats), our times will find men divided into two groups as well. One group will be productive, living out a life based in love and sacrifice to the needs of others. These men will be the ones who have found freedom from crippling sexual lust. This group of victorious men will supply the strength of leadership in families, churches, and in our broader society.

The second group will be the large mass of men who will simply give in to regular, daily, overpowering lust. These people will survive on constant doses of pornography and other sexually graphic images. And since unbridled sexual promiscuity (real or vicarious) zaps male productivity, this second group will be comprised of men who have lost power.

Samson lost strength when his hair was cut off. His hair was a symbol of his Nazarite oath, a commitment broken when the hair was shaved. The mass of men in the western world will miss the fulfillment of deep, meaningful relationships, and will substitute sexual lust for the empowering love that could otherwise await them. They will also lose their strength in the Lord when their vow of discipleship is broken.

John 8: 34-36 records these words of Jesus:

> *"Truly, truly, I say to you, every one who commits sin is a slave to sin. The slave does not continue in the house for ever; the Son continues for ever. So if the Son makes you free, you will be free indeed."*

It is my prayer at this time, dear reader, that you will be one of those men who struggles through to freedom from the sin of lust...a freedom which comes through the person and protection of Jesus Christ.

In summary, the key steps in the process of achieving that freedom are:

• Learn what lust is, and admit that it is sin.

• Admit that lust (sin) is a problem in your life.

• Condition yourself to recognize the very moment lust begins to appear in your mind and heart.

• Turn to the Lord through prayer (as often as needed, and without fail) for protection from the lust that would attack you.

• Begin finding some victories over lust through God's protection, and proclaim and celebrate those victories.

• Ask a close male friend to help hold you accountable in this area of your life (and/or join a sexual addiction support group).

• Discuss with your wife (or girlfriend) the problems you are having with lust.

• Build relationships, especially the one with your wife, along the unselfish lines our Creator intended.

• Do not tire of the process until you achieve freedom from lust.

• And finally, enjoy the life of love the Lord will give you.

"When you were slaves of sin, you were free in regard to righteousness. But then what return did you get from the things of which you are now ashamed? The end of those things is death. But now that you have been set free from sin and have become slaves of God, the return you get is sanctification and its end, eternal life. For the wages of sin is death, but the free gift of God is eternal life in Christ Jesus our Lord" (Romans 6: 20-23).

ABOUT THE AUTHOR

Pastor Wallace W. White leads the congregation at Valleyview Friends Church in Delaware, Ohio. A recorded Friends pastor, his work prior to the ministry included public library administration and journalism. He and "the wife of his youth" Carol have three grown children and five grandchildren.

0-595-24383-5

www.ingramcontent.com/pod-product-compliance
Lightning Source LLC
Chambersburg PA
CBHW031231280526
45784CB00004B/1531